外研社汉语分级读物——中文天天读
FLTRP Graded Readers — Reading China

小马过河
A Little Horse Crosses the River

1B

顾　问：魏崇新　张晓慧　吴丽君
主　编：朱勇
编　著：朱勇　黄芳　王凡　华晨
翻　译：王玉通

外语教学与研究出版社
FOREIGN LANGUAGE TEACHING AND RESEARCH PRESS
北京 BEIJING

图书在版编目（CIP）数据

小马过河：1B／朱勇等编著；王玉通译. —北京：外语教学与研究出版社，2011.5（2023.4重印）
（外研社汉语分级读物：中文天天读 ／ 朱勇主编）
ISBN 978-7-5135-0834-6

Ⅰ. ①小⋯ Ⅱ. ①朱⋯ ②王⋯ Ⅲ. ①汉语－对外汉语教学－语言读物 Ⅳ. ①H195.5

中国版本图书馆CIP数据核字(2011)第084891号

出 版 人	王　芳
选题策划	彭冬林　李彩霞
责任编辑	李彩霞　于　辉
英文编辑	蔡　莹
装帧设计	姚　军
插图绘制	北京碧悠动漫文化有限公司
出版发行	外语教学与研究出版社
社　　址	北京市西三环北路19号（100089）
网　　址	https://www.fltrp.com
印　　刷	北京虎彩文化传播有限公司
开　　本	830×1030　1/16
印　　张	7.5
版　　次	2011年6月第1版 2023年4月第4次印刷
书　　号	ISBN 978-7-5135-0834-6
定　　价	39.00元

如有图书采购需求，图书内容或印刷装订等问题，侵权、盗版书籍等线索，请拨打以下电话或关注官方服务号：
客服电话：400 898 7008
官方服务号：微信搜索并关注公众号"外研社官方服务号"
外研社购书网址：https://fltrp.tmall.com

物料号：208340001

编写说明

众所周知，阅读是成人外语学习者获得语言输入的重要方式。只有加强阅读，增加语言输入量，才能更快地学好一门外语。基于此，如何让学习者有效利用课余时间，通过快乐阅读、随意阅读来促进其语言学习，一直是众多语言教学与研究者所关注的课题之一。

令人遗憾的是，适合各种水平汉语学习者阅读需要的汉语分级读物，长期以来一直处于相对短缺的状态。鉴于此，外语教学与研究出版社2007年发起并组织编写了本套系列汉语分级读物——《中文天天读》，用于满足各级水平汉语学习者的阅读需求，让学习者在快乐阅读的同时有效提高自己的汉语水平。同时，也通过巧妙的关于中国社会、历史、文化背景的介绍与传达，为所有汉语学习者真正开启一扇了解当代中国的窗口。

《中文天天读》按语言难度分为5级，每级各有2个不同的分册，可适合不同级别的学习者使用。文章字数等具体说明请看下表。

级 别	文章字数	词汇量	篇 目	已学时间
1级	100～150	500	25篇	三个月（160学时）
2级	150～300	1000	25篇	半年（320学时）
3级	300～550	2000	25篇	一年（640学时）
4级	500～750	3500	20篇	两年（1280学时）
5级	700～1200	5000	18篇	三年（1920学时）

为方便更多语种的学习者学习，《中文天天读》将陆续出版英、日、韩、西、德、法、意、俄等十多种语言的版本，学习者可根据情况自选。

《中文天天读》大致有以下几个模块：

1. 阅读前模块——导读。导读主要是一两个跟文章有关的问题，类似于课堂导入，主要是激发学生的兴趣，起到热身的作用。

2. 阅读中模块，包括正文、边注、插图。边注是对生词进行随文对译和解释的一种方式，目的是帮助学习者扫清生词障碍，迅速获得词义。它有助于降低文章难度，保持阅读速度。插图也是《中文天天读》的一大特色。插图中反映的都是课文的核心内容，也经常出现课文中的关键句子。这些都有助于读者"见图知义"，快速理解课文内容。

3. 阅读后模块，包括语言点、练习和小知识。语言点是对重点词语或结构的简单说明。每个语言点的第一个例句大多是课文中的原句，其他例句的目的是帮助学生"温故而知新"，句子中着力使用已学课文中的生词或者语境。练习题的题型主要有问答题、选择题、判断题、填表题等，都和内容理解有关。《中文天天读》的题量不大，因为过多的练习会破坏阅读的乐趣。小知识中，有的是跟文章内容密切相关的背景知识，读了以后直接有助于理解课文；有的跟文章有一定关系，是对课文内容的补充和延伸；还有一种则属于一般性的中国文化、历史地理知识介绍。

与同类材料相比，《中文天天读》具有以下特点：

1. 易读易懂。"容易些，再容易些"是我们编写《中文天天读》一直持有的理念。对于每篇选文的生词、字数我们都有严格的控制。我们还通过为边注词、小知识等配以英、日、韩、西等不同语种译文的方式，方便学习者更好地理解课文。此外，每课均配有与课文、小知识内容匹配的漫画或图片，通过这些关键线索，唤起读者大脑中的相关图式，有效地起到助读的作用。

2. 多样有趣。"兴趣是最好的老师"，我们力求选文富有情趣。选文伊始，我们即根据已有经验以及相关调查，对留学生的需求进行了分析，尽可能保证选文在一定程度上能够投其所好。具体做法是：(1) 话题多样，内容丰富。这样可以保持阅读的新鲜感。

《中文天天读》各册从普通中国人的衣食住行、传统风俗与现代生活的交替到中国当代的社会、经济、语言、文化等内容均有涉及，有的还从中外对比的角度来叙述和分析，力求让读者了解到中国社会的真实面貌，同时还可以对学生的跨文化交际能力起到一定的指导作用；(2) 文体多样，形式活泼。《中文天天读》中，记叙文、说明文、议论文、书信、诗歌、小小说等文体不拘一格，让读者充分了解汉语的不同体裁，感受中文的魅力。

3. **注重实用**。选文比较实用，其中不少文章都贴近留学生的生活。有的文章本身就是一些有助于留学生在中国的学习、生活、旅行、工作的相关介绍，可以学以致用。

4. **听读结合**。《中文天天读》每册均配有相应的 CD 或 MP3，读者既可以通过"读"的方式欣赏地道的中文，也可以通过"听"的方式感受纯正的普通话。这两种输入方式会从不同的角度帮助学习者提高汉语水平。

在编写过程中，我们从阅读教学专家、全国对外汉语优秀教师刘颂浩先生那里获益良多；我的同事马晓冬博士提出了许多建设性的意见；外语教学与研究出版社汉语分社给予该项目以大力支持，李彩霞、李杨、庄晶晶、颜莉、于辉、许杨等编辑为《中文天天读》的策划、编写做出了特别贡献；北外中文学院2006级、2007级的10多位研究生在项目启动之初的选文方面也给我们很多帮助，在此一并致谢！

欢迎广大同行、读者批评指导，也欢迎大家将使用过程中发现的问题反馈给我们，以便再版时更上一层楼。联系方式：zhuyong1706@gmail.com。

朱勇

2010 年 12 月

Preface

It is common knowledge that reading is an important input channel for adult learners of a foreign language. Extensive reading can ensure adequate language input and fast, efficient learning. Therefore, both language researchers and teachers emphasize large amount of reading in addition to classroom learning.

Regrettably, well designed and appropriately graded reading materials for second-language learners are hard to come by. Aware of the shortage, the Foreign Language Teaching and Research Press initiated in 2007 the compilation of *Reading China*, a series of readers tailored to the diverse needs of learners at different levels of Chinese proficiency. The readers feature fun stories of present-day China, with introductions on Chinese history, culture and everyday life.

There are altogether five levels in the series, each consisting of two volumes. Please refer to the table below for specific data:

Level	Length of Texts (words)	Vocabulary	Number of Texts	Prior Chinese Learning
1	100~150	500	25	Three months (160 credit hours)
2	150~300	1000	25	Half a year (320 credit hours)
3	300~550	2000	25	One year (640 credit hours)
4	500~750	3500	20	Two years (1280 credit hours)
5	700~1200	5000	18	Three years (1920 credit hours)

Other language versions of the series, such as Japanese, Korean, Spanish, German,

French, Italian and Russian, will come off the press soon to facilitate the study of Chinese learners with these language backgrounds.

Each book of the series includes the following modules:

1. Pre-reading—Lead-in. This part has one or two interesting warming-up questions, which function as an introduction to a new text.

2. Reading—Texts, Side Notes and Illustrations. Side Notes provide equivalents and explanations for new words and expressions to help learners better understand the text. This part also keeps the degree of difficulty of the texts within reasonable bounds so that learners can read them at a reasonable speed. Illustrations are another highlight of the series. They help learners take in at a glance the key sentences and main ideas of the texts.

3. After-reading—Language Points, Exercises and Cultural Tips. The Language Points part hammers home the meaning and usage of important words and expressions, or grammar points in one of the sentences from the text. Two follow-up example sentences, usually with words, expressions or linguistic contexts from previous texts, are given to help learners "gain new insights through review of old materials". In Exercises, a small amount of questions, choice questions, true or false questions and cloze tests, are designed to check learners' comprehension of the texts without spoiling the fun of reading. In Cultural Tips, background information is provided as supplementary reading materials. Some are related to the texts and some are just general information about Chinese culture, history and geography.

Reading China stands out among similar readers because of the following features:

1. User-friendliness: "Reading should be as easy as possible", a principle consistently followed by the compilers, through strict control of the number of new words and expressions in each text, the Side Notes, the translations given in Language

Points and Cultural Tips, illustrations and pictures.

2. Diversity and fun: The compilers have taken great pains in choosing interesting stories because "interest is the best teacher". We also try to cater to foreign students' reading preferences by analyzing their learning expectations on the basis of our teaching experience and surveys. Firstly, a wide range of topics is included to sustain the freshness of reading. The stories touch upon many aspects of Chinese life. In some cases, similarities and differences between Chinese and foreign cultures are compared and analyzed to give learners a realistic idea about contemporary China and improve their cross-cultural communication ability. Secondly, different writing genres and styles are selected, such as narrations, instructions, argumentations, letters, poems, mini-stories, etc. In this way, learners can fully appreciate the charm of the Chinese language.

3. Practicality: Many texts are closely related to foreign students' life in China and contain practical information about studying, living, traveling and working in China.

4. Listening materials: MP3 or CDs are provided for each book of the series. Integration of audio input through listening and visual input through reading will further improve learning results.

In the course of our compilation work, we have benefited a great deal from the expertise of Mr. Liu Songhao, an expert in teaching Chinese reading and an excellent teacher of Chinese as a second language. Dr. Ma Xiaodong, my colleague, has provided many inspiring suggestions. Our heartfelt gratitude goes to the directors and editors of the FLTRP Chinese Publishing Division, in particular Li Caixia, Li Yang, Zhuang Jingjing, Yan Li, Yu Hui and Xu Yang, for their contribution to the planning and compilation of this series. We also wish to thank more than ten postgraduate students of the years 2006 and 2007 at BFSU for their help in collecting materials at the early stage of this project.

We would greatly appreciate suggestions and comments from learners and teachers of Chinese as a second language and would accordingly improve the books in the future. Contact information: zhuyong1706@gmail.com.

Zhu Yong
December, 2010

使用建议

感谢您关注并选用《中文天天读》！关于怎样更好地使用这套阅读资源，作为编者，我们在这里提出几点建议，供您参考。

一、教材选用

《中文天天读》是一套以"在快乐阅读中体验汉语并了解中国"为目的的分级读物。因为它每一册的容量都不太大，每一课都编配有语言点例释和练习，所以又可以作为专门的阅读教材来使用。

教师可以根据《中文天天读》"编写说明"中每一级在长度、词汇量、篇目等方面的信息，结合学习者的水平来选用相应级别的教材。《中文天天读》每一级又包括A、B2册，其难度为A<B。

二、课程进度

《中文天天读》纸质版本中每课的练习量都比较少，一般来说，2课时左右可以完成1-2篇课文的教学。如果是国内的长期教学，每周2-4课时的话，一学期可以完成两册书的教学。如果是短期教学或者在国外课时比较少的情况下，一个教学周期一般能完成一册书的教学。

三、教学过程

阅读前。《中文天天读》每一课的"导读"可以作为教师的导入语来使用,教师根据实际情况可以让学生进行简单的讨论;正文的插图也可以作为导入材料,让学生读前先看插图,通过插图来猜测课文反映的内容,这样课本就变成了一份看图说话的练习资料;教师也可以从听入手,在读前让学生听一遍配套的 CD 或 MP3。这样多种途径结合,可以充分调动学习者的阅读兴趣和相关的图式背景,为更好地理解阅读材料服务。

阅读中。可以综合运用默读、轮读、小组读、带着问题查读等多种形式,使学习者对阅读材料达到充分的感知。

阅读后。《中文天天读》的练习大致可以分为四种:课文理解题主要检测学习者对课文的理解程度;语言练习题、阅读技能训练题和写作题则可以帮助学习者积累语言知识,并提高读写技能。书中的小知识可以作为课堂阅读的补充,也可以作为课下阅读材料使用,教师可在其基础上适当作一些话题扩展,将语言学习与文化习得有机结合起来,让学生在不知不觉中伴随性地获得有关中国历史文化的知识。配套的 CD 或 MP3 也可以放在读后来听,以达到复习巩固的目的。

How to Use *Reading China*

Welcome to use *Reading China*! As the compiler, we would like to offer some suggestions concerning how to better make use of this set of reading materials.

1. How to choose books

Reading China is a set of graded reading materials targeting at "experiencing Chinese and understanding China through happy reading". Since the number of lessons in each book is not too much and each lesson is equipped with Language Points and Exercises, this series can be used as reading textbooks in class.

Teachers are advised to read the "Preface" at the beginning of the books for information on length of texts, vocabulary, and number of texts of each level of books, and choose the appropriate level for the learners. There are two volumes in each level of *Reading China* – A and B, and the level of difficulty is A<B.

2. How to make the schedule

The exercises for each lesson in *Reading China* are not too much. Generally speaking, one to two texts can be finished in a two-hour class. For long-term training programs in China, two books can be covered in a semester if there are two to four class hours in a week; for short-term training programs or overseas programs, one book can be covered in a teaching session.

3. How to teach with this series

Pre-reading: Teachers can develop their own class introductions on the basis of Lead-in at the beginning of each lesson and think of some topics for discussions for students. On the one hand, with the help of Illustrations, students can look at the pictures before reading the texts to guess what the text is about. In this way, the series become exercise materials for "look and say" practices. On the other hand, with the help of CD or MP3, students can listen to the recording before reading the texts to get a general idea. A combination of different methods can effectively activate learners' interest in reading and enhance their knowledge of the background, so as to better help with their understanding of the texts.

Reading: There are a variety of ways of reading the texts, such as silent reading, reading in pairs, reading in groups, reading with questions in mind, through which learners can acquire an adequate perception of the reading materials.

After-reading: There are four types of exercises in *Reading China*. Apprehension questions examine learners' understanding of the texts. Language practice, reading skill trainings and writing tasks help learners accumulate knowledge about the language and improve their skill of reading and writing. Cultural Tips can serve as the extension of in-class reading or as after school reading materials. Teachers may further explore the topics to integrate language learning with cultural acquisition, so that students can acquire more knowledge about China's history and culture in an easy and interesting way. Students can listen to CD or MP3 after reading the texts to consolidate what has been learned.

目录
Contents

1 小心地滑
Caution: Slippery Floor / 14

2 "妈妈"的电话
A Call from a "Mother" / 18

3 教师节快乐
Happy Teachers' Day / 22

4 我叫马西文
My Name Is Ma Xiwen / 26

5 我是ABC
I'm an "ABC" / 30

6 美人？没人？
Pretty One? No one? / 34

7 怎么回家
How to Get Back Home / 38

8 果然
Sure Enough / 42

9 方向错了
The Wrong Direction / 46

10 座位在哪里？
Finding the Seats / 50

11 小声一点儿
Hush… / 54

12 走错了
The Wrong Door / 58

13 手机丢了
Lost Mobile Phone / 62

14 古老的城市——西安
The Ancient City of Xi'an / 66

15 漂亮的一"点"
The Highlight / 70

16 通知
Notice / 74

17 冰糖葫芦
Sugar-Coated Haws / 78

18 马大哈
A Scatterbrain / 82

19 小马过河
A Little Horse Crosses the River / 86

20 一点儿
Just a Little Bit / 90

21 前门 ≠ 前门儿
The Tricky Suffix of "R" / 94

22 多变的气候
A Varied Climate / 98

23 长生果
Elixir of Life / 102

24 我看见了大熊猫
Seeing Pandas / 106

25 我开博客了
Starting a Blog / 110

练习答案
Answer Keys / 114

1 小心地滑
Xiǎoxīn dì huá
Caution: Slippery Floor

今天是星期天。杰克和他的中国朋友李小明去逛商场。杰克一进商场就开始滑着走。

一不小心,杰克滑倒了。

小明觉得很奇怪,就问杰克:

"你为什么滑着走呢?"

| 小心地滑　Caution: Slippery Floor

Jiékè zhǐzhe dìshang de páizi shuō: "Zhèlǐ
杰克指着地上的牌子说："这里

xiězhe 'xiǎoxīn de huá', wǒ fēicháng xiǎoxīn,
写着'小心地 滑'，我 非常 小心，

kě háishì huádǎo le."
可还是滑倒了。"

Xiǎomíng dàxiào: "Shì 'xiǎoxīn dì huá',
小明 大笑："是'小心地滑'，

búshì 'xiǎoxīn de huá'."
不是'小心地滑'。"

逛 v. stroll	奇怪 adj. curious
商场 n. market, shopping mall	指 v. point to
开始 v. start, begin	牌子 n. sign
滑 v. slide, slip	笑 v. smile, laugh

语言点 Language Points

一不小心
carelessly, by accident

1. 一不小心，杰克突然滑倒了。

   "一不小心"，跟"不小心"意思相同，表示不注意、不留神。

   "一不小心" or "不小心" means "carelessly, by accident".

   (1) 雨很大，西川一不小心滑倒了。

   (2) 今天很冷，小明一不小心感冒了。

觉得
think

2. 小明觉得很奇怪，就问杰克。

   "觉得"，动词。表示认为的意思，常用来说出自己的想法。

   "觉得" is a verb. It means "somebody thinks that...", and is often used to express opinions.

   (1) 我觉得那个女生很漂亮。

   (2) 我觉得你的汉语很好。

练习 Exercises

1. 判断正误。True or false.

   (1) 今天是星期六。   (   )

   (2) 杰克和李小明是同学。   (   )

2. 选择正确答案。Choose the correct answer.

（1）杰克滑倒了，是因为他（　　）。

　　A. 不小心　　　　　B. 汉语不太好　　　　C. 汉语太好了

（2）"小心地滑"的"地"读音是（　　）。

　　A. dì　　　　　　　B. de　　　　　　　　C. dī

小知识 Cultural Tips

"和"字的五种读音
The Five Pronunciations of "和"

　　汉语里有不少多音字，这些不同的读音常常表达不同的意思，因此也是学习汉语的难点之一。比如"和"字就有 hé、hè、hú、huó、huò 五个音，对应的词语分别是：我和 (hé) 你、附和 (hè)、牌和 (hú) 了、和 (huó) 面、和 (huò) 稀泥。

There are many polyphones in the Chinese language. Different pronunciations often have their particular meanings, thus posing challenges for learners of Chinese. Take the character of "和" as an example. It has five pronunciations: hé, hè, hú, huó, and huò, and each is used in such ways as "我和(hé)你", "附和(hè)", "牌和(hú)了", "和(huó)面", and "和(huò)稀泥".

2 "妈妈"的电话
"Māma" de diànhuà
A Call from a "Mother"

Xiǎoxuě fēicháng xǐhuan kàn Chénglóng de
小雪 非常 喜欢 看 成龙 的

diànyǐng, tā shì yí ge "Chénglóng mí."
电影，她是一个"成龙 迷。"

Jīntiān wǎnshang, Chénglóng yào lái Běijīng
今天 晚上， 成龙 要来北京

hé yǐngmí jiànmiàn, Xiǎoxuě fēicháng xiǎng qù.
和影迷见面，小雪 非常 想 去。

Dàn jiànmiànhuì shì shàngkè de shíjiān.
但 见面会 是 上课 的 时间。

2 "妈妈"的电话 A Call from a "Mother"

Wèile jiàndào Chénglóng, tā xiǎng
为了见到成龙，她想

qǐngjià, búqù shàngkè le.
请假，不去上课了。

Xiǎoxuě xiǎngle xiǎng, jiù gěi lǎoshī dǎ
小雪想了想，就给老师打

diànhuà le: "Lǎoshī, nín hǎo, Xiǎoxuě
电话了："老师，您好，小雪

jīntiān shēngbìng le, bùnéng qù shàngkè le."
今天生病了，不能去上课了。"

Lǎoshī wèn "Nǐ shì ……?"
老师问"你是……？"

"Wǒ shì wǒ māma."
"我是我妈妈。"

喜欢 v. like, love	为了 prep. in order to	生病 v. get sick
电影 n. movie	请假 v. ask for leave	能 v. can, be able to
见面会 n. fan meeting		

语言点 Language Points

迷
fan, enthusiast

1. 小雪是一个"成龙迷"。

   "迷",名词。表示特别喜欢某事或某物的人。

   "迷" is a noun, which refers to somebody who admires something or somebody.

   (1) 小王非常喜欢汽车,是一个"汽车迷"。
   (2) 杰克是一个"电影迷",他每天都要看电影。

见面
meet

2. 成龙要来北京和影迷见面。

   "见面",动词。表示双方相见,常用"和……见面"。

   "见面" is a verb. It means "to meet each other", often used in "和……见面".

   (1) 他和女朋友的第一次见面是在 2008 年 8 月 8 日。
   (2) 李小明和杰克明天下午 3 点见面,他们要去逛商场。

练习 Exercises

1. 判断正误。True or false.

   (1) 小雪很喜欢成龙的电影。　　　　　　　　　　　　(　　)
   (2) 小雪妈妈给老师打电话请假。　　　　　　　　　　(　　)

2. 选择正确答案。 Choose the correct answer.

（1）小雪给老师打电话，是因为她（　　）。

　　A. 生病了　　　　　　　B. 想看电影　　　　　　C. 想参加成龙的见面会

（2）小雪说"我是我妈妈"后，老师可能会说（　　）。

　　A. 小雪的妈妈，你好　　B. 你是小雪　　　　　　C. 好的

小知识　Cultural Tips

成龙
Jackie Chan

　　成龙，1954年生于中国香港，英文名Jackie Chan，功夫电影巨星。代表作有《醉拳》、《警察故事》、《A计划》和《尖峰时刻》等。他还热心于慈善事业和公益事业，是一位爱心大使。

　　Jackie Chan, a well-known Kung Fu and action movie star, was born in the year 1954 in Hong Kong, China. Chan starred in *Drunken Master, Police Story, Project A, Rush Hour,* and many other movies. As a goodwill ambassador, he is also an enthusiastic supporter of charities and public welfare undertakings.

3 Jiàoshījié kuàilè
教师节快乐
Happy Teachers' Day

Yì zhāng míngxìnpiàn
一张 明信片

Qīn'ài de lǎoshī:
亲爱的老师：

Nín hǎo!
您好！

Jīntiān shì 9 yuè 10 rì, Zhōngguó de jiàoshījié. Xièxie nín jiāo wǒmen hànyǔ,
今天是9月10日，中国的教师节。谢谢您教我们汉语，

jiāo wǒmen zhōngwéngē. Zhù nín jiérì kuàilè!
教我们中文歌。祝您节日快乐！

Nín de xuéshēng: Lǐ Měizǐ
您的学生：李美子

2010 nián 9 yuè 10 rì
2010年9月10日

3 教师节快乐 Happy Teachers' Day

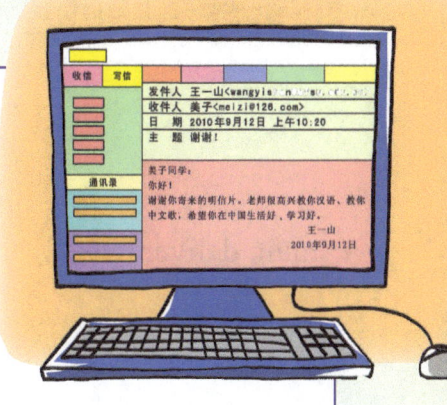

Yì fēng Email
一封 Email

发件人 *fājiànrén*	Wáng Yīshān　　<wangyishan@bfsu.edu.cn> 王　一山<wangyishan@bfsu.edu.cn>
收件人 *shōujiànrén*	Měizǐ　　<meizi@126.com> 美子<meizi@126.com>
日期 *rìqī*	2010 nián 9 yuè 12 rì shàngwǔ 10:20 2010年9月12日 上午 10:20
主题 *zhǔtí*	Xièxie ! 谢谢！

Měizǐ tóngxué
美子同学：

　　Nǐ hǎo!
　　你 好！

　　Xièxie nǐ jìlái de míngxìnpiàn. Lǎoshī hěn gāoxìng jiāo nǐ hànyǔ, jiāo nǐ zhōngwén-
　　谢谢你寄来的明信片。老师 很 高兴 教你汉语，教你 中文

gē, xīwàng nǐ zài Zhōngguó shēnghuó hǎo, xuéxí hǎo.
歌，希望你在 中国 生活 好、学习好。

Wáng Yīshān
王　一山

2010 nián 9 yuè 12 rì
2010年9月12日

明信片 *n.* postcard　　　　教 *v.* teach　　　　　　节日 *n.* holiday, festival
亲爱的 dear　　　　　　　歌 *n.* song　　　　　　生活 *v.* live
您 *pron.* you　　　　　　 祝 *v.* wish

23

语言点 Language Points

寄 — mail, deliver by post

1. 谢谢你寄来的明信片。

   "寄",动词。把邮件交给邮局,通过邮局传递给收件人。

   "寄" is a verb. It means "to mail", i.e. to deliver something to somebody by post.

   (1) 为了祝王老师教师节快乐,我给她寄了一张明信片。

   (2) 来中国一个月了,明天我要给爸爸妈妈寄一封信。

希望 — hope, wish for

2. 希望你在中国生活好、学习好。

   "希望",动词。心里想着实现某种愿望。

   "希望" is a verb, which means "to hope..." or "to wish for...".

   (1) 小雪希望能去成龙的影迷见面会。

   (2) 我们希望王老师教我们汉语。

练习 Exercises

1. 判断正误。True or false.

   (1) 王一山给美子寄了一张明信片。　　　　　　　　　　　　(　　)

   (2) 9月10日是中国的教师节。　　　　　　　　　　　　　　(　　)

   (3) 王老师很高兴教美子中文歌。　　　　　　　　　　　　　(　　)

3 教师节快乐 Happy Teachers' Day

2. 选择正确答案。Choose the correct answer.

(1) 教（　）汉语　　　教（　）师　　　教（　）中文歌

　　A. jiāo　　　　　　B. jiào

(2) 一（　）明信片　　一（　）Email　　一（　）信

　　A. 封　　　　　　　B. 张

小知识 Cultural Tips

中国的教师节
Teachers' Day in China

尊敬教师是中华民族的优良传统。1985年1月中国将每年的9月10日定为教师节。之所以确定9月10日为教师节，是因为新生刚刚入学，尊师重教可以给教师教好、学生学好创造良好的氛围。同时，9月份节日少，便于突出教师节。

To honor the long-cherished Chinese tradition of showing respect to teachers, September 10 was established to be the Teachers' Day in China in January, 1985. The reason to choose this day is because it is around the beginning of the fall semester, and honoring teachers helps to create a sound atmosphere of teaching and learning. Meanwhile, September has few national celebrations, making it easy to focus on Teachers' Day.

4 我叫马西文
Wǒ jiào Mǎ Xīwén
My Name Is Ma Xiwen

大家好！现在自我介绍一下，
Dàjiā hǎo! Xiànzài zìwǒ jièshào yíxià,

我的名字叫马西文，是美国人。
wǒ de míngzi jiào Mǎ Xīwén, shì Měiguórén.

我喜欢唱歌、游泳。到中国
Wǒ xǐhuan chànggē, yóuyǒng. Dào Zhōngguó

以后，也开始喜欢打乒乓球了。
yǐhòu, yě kāishǐ xǐhuan dǎ pīngpāngqiú le.

你们好！我是日本人，我的
Nǐmen hǎo! Wǒ shì Rìběnrén, wǒ de

名字叫西川，我最喜欢的运动
míngzi jiào Xīchuān, wǒ zuì xǐhuan de yùndòng

是骑自行车。你们呢？
shì qí zìxíngchē. Nǐmen ne?

4 我叫马西文 My Name Is Ma Xiwen

Tóngxuémen hǎo! Wǒ jiào Lǐ Měizǐ, shì
同学们 好！我 叫李美子，是
Hánguórén. Wǒ xǐhuan Zhōngguócài, yǐhòu
韩国人。我 喜欢 中国 菜，以后
wǒmen kěyǐ yìqǐ chīfàn.
我们 可以一起吃饭。

Péngyoumen, wǒ shì Mǎlì, Fǎguórén.
朋友们，我是玛丽，法国人。
Hěn gāoxìng rènshi dàjiā, xīwàng wǒmen hěnkuài
很 高兴 认识大家，希望 我们 很快
chéngwéi hǎo péngyou.
成为 好 朋友。

大家 *pron.* everybody	运动 *n.* sports
自我介绍 introduce oneself	骑 *v.* ride
唱歌 *v.* sing	自行车 *n.* bicycle, bike
游泳 *v.* swim	成为 *v.* become
乒乓球 *n.* table tennis, ping-pong	

中文天天读 Reading China

语言点 Language Points

介绍
introduce

1. 现在自我介绍一下，我的名字叫马西文。

   "介绍"，动词。意思是告知别人他们不知道的信息。

   "介绍" is a verb, which means "to introduce", or to provide information that the listeners do not know.

   (1) 大家好！介绍一下，这是我的好朋友玛丽。
   (2) 同学们，你们介绍一下自己的名字好吗？

认识
know

2. 很高兴认识大家，希望我们很快成为好朋友。

   "认识"，动词。表示能够确定这一人或事物不是别的人或事物。

   "认识" is a verb, which means to identify something or somebody from others.

   (1) 我和山本都是日本人，我们很早就认识了。
   (2) 李美子是我的同学，我们已经认识三天了。

4 我叫马西文 My Name Is Ma Xiwen

练习 Exercises

连线。Match.

西川　　　　美国人　　　　喜欢中国菜

马西文　　　韩国人　　　　喜欢游泳

李美子　　　法国人　　　　喜欢骑自行车

玛丽　　　　日本人　　　　喜欢打乒乓球

小知识 Cultural Tips

哪些国家使用过汉字？
In Which Countries Were Chinese Characters Used?

历史上，中国的几个周边国家都曾经使用过汉字，它们是日本、朝鲜、韩国和越南等国。其中，日本到现在仍然使用汉字，日语中的常用汉字有2,000个左右。

Chinese characters were once used in China's neighboring countries such as Japan, DPRK, ROK and Vietnam in history, and the Japanese language today still has around 2,000 frequently-used Chinese characters.

5 我是ABC

Wǒ shì A B C

I'm an "ABC"

Wǒ bàba shì Měiguórén, māma shì
我爸爸是美国人，妈妈是

Zhōngguórén, dàjiā dōu shuō wǒ shì ABC
中国人，大家都说我是ABC

(American Born Chinese). Māma de
(American Born Chinese)。妈妈的

lǎojiā zài Shànghǎi, wàigōng hé wàipó xiànzài hái
老家在上海，外公和外婆现在还

zhùzài Shànghǎi.
住在上海。

Wǒ xiǎoshíhou gēn bàba māma yìqǐ
我小时候跟爸爸妈妈一起

qùguò Shànghǎi, dàn nà shì shí nián yǐqián
去过上海，但那是十年以前

de shìqing le.
的事情了。

5 我是ABC *I'm an "ABC"*

Xuéxiào hěn kuài jiù fàng shǔjià le, wǒ fēicháng xiǎng zǎodiǎnr qù Shànghǎi.
学校 很 快 就 放 暑假 了，我 非常 想 早点儿去 上海。

Wèishénme ne? Yīnwèi wǒ hěn xǐhuan wàipó zuò de Zhōngguócài, háiyǒu jīnnián de
为什么 呢？因为我很喜欢外婆做的 中国菜，还有今年的

Shìbóhuì zài Shànghǎi jǔxíng, nàlǐ yídìng fēicháng yǒu yìsi.
世博会在 上海 举行，那里一定 非常 有意思。

Nǐ bù xiǎng qù ma?
你不 想 去吗？

老家 *n.* hometown	住 *v.* live	菜 *n.* cuisine
外公 *n.* grandfather	以前 *n.* ago, earlier times	世博会 World Expo
外婆 *n.* grandmother	暑假 *n.* summer holiday	一定 *adv.* surely

文天天读 Reading China

语言点 Language Points

举行
hold, have

1. 今年的世博会在上海举行。

   "举行",动词。进行(比赛、活动)。

   "举行" is a verb, which means "to hold (a competition, an event, etc.)".

   (1) 你知道2015年世博会在哪儿举行吗?

   (2) 成龙影迷见面会明天在北京举行。

还有
also, too,
as well,
in addition

2. 我很喜欢中国菜,还有世博会在上海举行,那里一定非常有意思。

   "还有",连词。常用来进行补充说明,表示除了已经说的,还有别的。

   "还有" is a conjunction. It is often used to make additional explanations, and it expresses that in addition to what has already been said, there is something else.

   (1) 马西文喜欢游泳、骑自行车,还有打乒乓球。

   (2) 我每天都上汉语课,还有学中文歌,很有意思。

练 习 Exercises

1. 判断正误。True or false.

   (1) 我没去过上海。   (   )

   (2) 今年的世博会在上海举行。   (   )

   (3) 我放暑假以后就去上海。   (   )

   (4) 我喜欢外婆做的中国菜。   (   )

2. 填表。Fill in the form.

	出生地（Place of birth）	居住地（Residence）
我		美国
妈妈		美国
外婆	中国	

小知识 Cultural Tips

上海世博会
World Expo 2010 Shanghai China

上海世博会于2010年5月1日至10月31日在上海举行，主题是"城市，让生活更美好"。上海世博会会徽以中国汉字"世"字书法创意为形，表达世博会"理解、沟通、欢聚、合作"的理念。

The World Expo 2010 Shanghai China, themed with "Better City, Better Life", was held from May 1 to October 31, 2010 in Shanghai. The emblem, drawing from the Chinese character "世" which stands for "world", perfectly expresses the philosophies of Shanghai Expo, "understanding, communication, togetherness and cooperation".

6 Měirén? méirén?
美人？没人？
Pretty One? No one?

Fāngfang hěn xǐhuan Zhāng Xiǎolè, kěshì
芳芳 很 喜欢 张 小乐，可是

Xiǎolè bù zhīdào. Yìtiān zǎoshang, Fāngfang
小乐 不 知道。一天 早上， 芳芳

qǐchuáng yǐhòu, kànjiàn yì tiáo duǎnxìn:
起床 以后，看见 一 条 短信：

9 diǎn qù zhǎo nǐ, měirén. Xiǎolè.
9 点 去 找 你， 美 人。 小 乐。

Fāngfang fēicháng gāoxìng!
芳芳 非常 高兴！

Zhètiān, Fāngfang méiyǒu chūqù,
这天， 芳芳 没有 出去，

cóng zǎoshang děngdào xiàwǔ, kěshì
从 早上 等到 下午，可是

Xiǎolè què méi lái.
小乐 却 没 来。

6 美人？没人？ Pretty One? No one?

Fāngfang hěn shēngqì, tā gěi Xiǎolè dǎ
芳芳 很 生气，她给小乐打

diànhuà: "Nǐ wèishénme méi lái zhǎo wǒ?"
电话："你为什么没来找我？"

Xiǎolè shuō: "Wǒ zuótiān wǎnshang 9 diǎn qù
小乐说："我 昨天 晚上 9 点去

zhǎo nǐ le, nǐ jiā méirén ā!"
找 你了，你家没人 啊！"

Fāngfang gěi Xiǎolè kànle yíxià shǒujī,
芳芳 给小乐看了一下手机，

yuánlái zuótiān Xiǎolè bǎ "méirén" xiěchéng
原来 昨天小乐把"没人" 写成

le "měirén".
了"美人"。

起床 v. get up	等 v. wait
短信 n. text message	生气 v. get mad, get angry
从 prep. from	原来 adv. it turns out that
早上 n. morning	

35

> 文天天读 Reading China

语言点 Language Points

以后
afterwards, later

1. 芳芳起床以后，看见一条短信。

"以后"，名词。比现在或者某个时间晚的时间（和"以前"相对）。

"以后" is a noun, which refers to the time later than the present time or a particular time (opposite to "以前").

(1) 三天以前我在南京，现在在上海，四天以后去北京。

(2) 爸爸来中国以后，非常喜欢吃中国菜。

V. + 成
verb + 成

2. 原来昨天小乐把"没人"写成了"美人"。

"V. + 成"，表示成了别的，"成"表示结果。

"V. +成" means having done something unexpectedly. "成" is followed with the effect or result.

(1) 他一不小心，把"大"写成了"太"。

(2) 杰克把"小心地（dì）滑"看成了"小心地（de）滑"，所以在商场里滑倒了。

练 习 Exercises

1. 判断正误。True or false.

(1) 张小乐喜欢芳芳。　　　　　　　　　　　　　　　　（　）

(2) 张小乐昨天去找芳芳了。　　　　　　　　　　　　　（　）

2. 选择正确答案。Choose the correct answer.

(1) 小乐昨天晚上（　　）去找芳芳了。

　　A. 7 点　　　　　　B. 8 点　　　　　　C. 9 点

(2) 芳芳为什么生气？（　　）。

　　A. 小乐不喜欢她　　B. 小乐没给她打电话　　C. 小乐今天没来找她

小知识 Cultural Tips

姓名叠音
Reiterative Words in Names

现在中国人起的小名常常是叠音词：田田、园园、飞飞、聪聪。不过，不少人的大名也采用叠音：(李) 芳芳、(张) 京京、(王) 天天。而以前无论是小名还是大名，很多人都喜欢用"小……"，比如说：小明、小强、(张) 小天、(赵) 小乐。

Nowadays, reiterative words appear not only in many Chinese babies' childhood names, such as 田田, 园园, 飞飞, and 聪聪, but also in many adults' formal names like (李)芳芳, (张)京京, and (王)天天. In the past, however, people tend to add "小" into childhood names and formal names as well, and some examples are: 小明, 小强, (张)小天, and (赵)小乐.

7 怎么回家
Zěnme huíjiā
How to Get Back Home

Yí gè pàngzi qù kàn yīshēng, wèn yǒu shénme hǎo bànfǎ kěyǐ jiǎnféi.
一个胖子去看医生，问有什么好办法可以减肥。

Yīshēng shuō:"Duō chī shūcài hé shuǐguǒ, měi tiān chīwán fàn yǐhòu zǒu 5 gōnglǐ. Sān gè yuè yǐhòu zài gěi wǒ dǎ diànhuà."
医生说：“多吃蔬菜和水果，每天吃完饭以后走5公里。三个月以后再给我打电话。”

7 怎么回家 How to Get Back Home

Sān gè yuè yǐhòu, zhè gè pàngzi gěi
三个月以后，这个胖子给
yīshēng dǎ diànhuà: "Gàosu nín yí gè hǎo
医生 打电话："告诉您一个好
xiāoxi! Wǒ yǐjīng bú pàng le."
消息！我已经不胖了。"
Yīshēng hěn gāoxìng, shuō: "Tài hǎo
医生 很 高兴，说："太好
le!"
了！"

Pàngzi jiēzhe shuō: "Kěshì wǒ
胖子接着说："可是我
xiànzài zài 500 gōnglǐ yǐwài, wǒ zěnme
现在在500公里以外，我怎么
huíjiā ne?"
回家 呢？"

胖子 n. fat person	蔬菜 n. vegetable	消息 n. news
医生 n. doctor	水果 n. fruit	已经 adv. already
减肥 v. lose weight	告诉 v. tell	接着 adv. go on

文天天读 Reading China

语言点 Language Points

怎么 how

1. 我**怎么**回家呢?

   "怎么"，代词。询问方式、原因、性质、情况等。

   "怎么" is a pronoun, often used to ask about style, reason, nature, state of affairs, etc.

   (1) 胖子问医生："我**怎么**减肥呢？"
   (2) 老师，这个字**怎么**写？

以外 beyond, outside, other than, except

2. 我现在在500公里**以外**。

   "以外"，名词。不在某个范围的界限里（和"以内"相对）。

   "以外" is a noun, referring to the state of not being within a particular limit (opposite to "以内").

   (1) 到中国以后，我还没去过上海**以外**的地方呢。
   (2) 我家在北京的四环（4th Ring Road）**以外**。

练习 Exercises

1. 判断正误。True or false.

   (1) 医生让胖子每天运动。　　　　　　　　　　　　　　　　（　　）
   (2) 胖子现在不胖了。　　　　　　　　　　　　　　　　　　（　　）

7 怎么回家 How to Get Back Home

2. 选择正确答案。Choose the correct answer.

（1）胖子是怎么减肥的？他每天（　　）。

　　A. 不吃东西　　　　B. 多吃蔬菜、水果，走 5 公里　　　C. 走 500 公里

（2）医生让胖子（　　）以后给他打电话。

　　A. 一个月　　　　　B. 三个月　　　　　C. 五个月

小知识 Cultural Tips

中国传统的计量单位
Traditional Chinese Units of Measurement

中国有自己传统的计量单位。重量单位有"两"、"斤"、"公斤"，1 公斤 =2 斤，1 斤 =10 两，1 公斤 =1 千克。长度单位有"里"、"公里"，1 公里 =2 里。在生活中，人们还是习惯使用传统计量单位。

China has its traditional units of measurement. Among all the traditional mass units, "两"、"斤" and "公斤" are often used today：1公斤=2斤，1斤=10两, and 1公斤=1kilogram. Traditional units of length include "里"、"公里", etc., and 1公里=2里. In Chinese people's daily life, they often tend to use these traditional units of measurement.

8 果然
Guǒrán
Sure Enough

Qīngshuǐ shì Rìběnrén, tā zài Zhōngguó
清水是日本人，他在中国
liúxué yǐjīng liǎng gè duō yuè le. Tā xuéxí
留学已经两个多月了。他学习
hěn nǔlì, chéngjì yě hěn hǎo, dàn yǒushíhou
很努力，成绩也很好，但有时候
yě hěn tiáopí. Yí gè Xīngqī'èr de xiàwǔ,
也很调皮。一个星期二的下午，
Qīngshuǐ zhèngzài shàng hànyǔ kè, xuéxí "guǒrán" zhè gè cí.
清水正在上汉语课，学习"果然"这个词。

Lǎoshī shuō: "Qīngshuǐ, qǐng nǐ yòng
老师说："清水，请你用
'guǒrán' zhè gè cí zàojù."
'果然'这个词造句。"

8 果然 Sure Enough

Qīngshuǐ shuō:"Xiān chī shuǐ'guǒ',
清水 说:"先吃水'果',
'rán' hòu zài……"
'然'后再……"

Lǎoshī shuō:"Búduì, búduì,'guǒ'
老师 说:"不对,不对,'果'
hé 'rán' liǎng gè zì bùnéng fēnkāi!"
和'然'两个字不能分开!"

Qīngshuǐ shuō:"Lǎoshī, bié zháojí,
清水 说:"老师,别着急,
wǒ hái méiyǒu shuōwán ne. Xiān chī shuǐguǒ,
我还没有 说完 呢。先吃水果,
ránhòu zài hē kělè, guǒrán hěn shūfu."
然后再喝 可乐,果然 很舒服。"

努力 *adj.* hard-working	先 *adv.* first
成绩 *n.* academic record	然后 *conj.* then
调皮 *adj.* naughty	着急 *adj.* worried
用 *v.* use	舒服 *adj.* comfortable

语言点 Language Points

分开
separate, part

1. '果'和'然'两个字不能分开！

   "分开"，动词。人或物不在一起了。

   "分开" is a verb, which means people or things are no longer together.

   (1) 小雪和外公外婆分开一年了，她很想他们。
   (2) 要回国了，他不想和朋友们分开。

果然
sure enough

2. 先吃水果，然后再喝可乐，果然很舒服。

   "果然"，副词。表示事情的发展与事先所说的或所想象的一样。

   "果然" is an adverb, which expresses that things go just as it was said or expected before.

   (1) 天气预报 (weather forecast) 说今天下雨，果然下雨了。
   (2) 每天多吃水果和蔬菜，多运动，果然可以减肥！

练 习 Exercises

1. 判断正误。True or false.

   (1) 清水在日本留学两个月了。　　　　　　　　　　　　　(　　)
   (2) 清水不会用"果然"造句。　　　　　　　　　　　　　　(　　)

2. 选择并完成句子。Choose and complete the sentences.

(1) 老师（　　），很着急。

　　A. 不喜欢清水　　　B. 觉得清水说错了　　　C. 生气了

(2) 清水学习很努力，（　　）成绩很好，（　　）有时候也很调皮。

　　A. 因为　　　　　　B. 所以　　　　　　　　C. 但是

小知识 Cultural Tips

汉语的字和词

Characters and Words in the Chinese Language

汉语中的字，有的是词，比如"水"；有的不是词，它必须跟别的字（或者词）连在一起才能成为词，比如："果"。它自己不是一个词，跟"水"一起是一个词——"水果"，跟"然"一起也是一个词——"果然"。

Some characters in the Chinese Language are words, such as "水"; some are not, and can only be used in collocation with other characters or words, and "果" is a good example: put together with "水" or "然", it makes "水果" or "果然" respectively, both of which are words.

9 方向错了
Fāngxiàng cuò le
The Wrong Direction

Qùnián shǔjià, Wáng Míngming qù
去年暑假，王 明明 去
Hángzhōu lǚxíng. Hángzhōu hěn piàoliang,
杭州 旅行。杭州 很 漂亮，
tā qùle hěnduō dìfang, huāle bùshǎo qián.
他去了很多地方，花了不少 钱。

Yǒu yìtiān, tā shēnshang zhǐyǒu sān yuán
有一天，他 身上 只有 三 元
qián le.
钱了。

Tā zài gōnggòng qìchē zhàn wèn shòupiàoyuán:
他在 公共 汽车站 问 售票员：
"Cóng zhèlǐ dào Xī Hú duōshao qián?" Shòupiàoyuán
"从 这里到西湖 多少 钱？" 售票员
huídá: "Sì yuán." Tā xiǎng: "Wǒ zhǐyǒu sān yuán qián le, zìjǐ pǎo yíhuìr zài zuò
回答："四元。"他想："我 只有 三 元 钱了，自己跑一会儿再坐
chē ba."
车吧。"

9 方向错了 The Wrong Direction

Tā pǎole hěn cháng shíjiān, zhōngyú
他跑了很长时间，终于
zhuīshàng le nà liàng gōnggòng qìchē.
追上了那辆公共汽车。

Tā yòu wèn shòupiàoyuán: "Zhèlǐ dào
他又问售票员："这里到
Xī Hú duōshao qián?"
西湖多少钱？"

"Wǔ yuán."
"五元。"

"Tiān na, fāngxiàng cuò le!"
"天哪，方向错了！"

旅行 v. travel, go on a trip
地方 n. place
花 v. spend
售票员 n. bus conductor

跑 v. run
时间 n. time
天哪 Dear me!

47

中 文天天读 Reading China

语言点 Language Points

终于
finally, at last

1. 他跑了很长时间，终于追上了那辆公共汽车。

   "终于"，副词。表示经过比较长的时间或过程之后，出现了希望得到的结果。

   "终于" is an adverb, which expresses that after a long time or process, things go as one wishes.

   (1) 明天暑假就开始了，我终于可以去上海了！
   (2) 胖子每天吃完饭以后走5公里，3个月后终于减肥了！

追上
catch up with

2. 终于追上了那辆公共汽车。

   "追上"，"上"表示追的结果。

   In "追上"，"上" expresses the result of the action of "追".

   (1) 他终于追上了前面的人，是第一名！
   (2) 小明没追上公共汽车，很着急。

练习 Exercises

1. 判断正误。True or false.

   (1) 售票员骗（cheat）了王明明。　　　　　　　　　　　　（　　）
   (2) 王明明跑错方向了。　　　　　　　　　　　　　　　　（　　）

2. 选择正确答案。Choose the correct answer.

(1) 王明明想（　　）去西湖。

　　A. 跑步　　　　　　B. 走路　　　　　　C. 坐公共汽车

(2) 王明明先跑一会儿，然后再坐公共汽车，是因为（　　）。

　　A. 西湖很近　　　　B. 他的钱不够了　　　C. 车票太贵了

小知识　Cultural Tips

上有天堂，下有苏杭
Heaven Above, Suzhou and Hangzhou Below

苏州在江苏省，杭州在浙江省，它们都是中国著名的旅游城市。"上有天堂，下有苏杭"是说，苏州和杭州很美丽，和天堂一样美。人们常用这句话来形容苏州和杭州的美丽、富饶。

As China's renowned tourist cities, Suzhou is located in Jiangsu Province, and Hangzhou, Zhejiang Province. As the saying goes, "Heaven above, Suzhou and Hangzhou below", which means the two cities are as beautiful as heaven, and it is often used to describe the two cities' beauty and prosperity.

10 座位在哪里？
Zuòwèi zài nǎlǐ?
Finding the Seats

Qián Xiǎoxuě shì Nánjīng Dàxué de liúxuéshēng, bānshang yǒu 12 wèi tóngxué, 6 wèi
钱小雪是南京大学的留学生，班上有12位同学，6位
nánshēng, 6 wèi nǚshēng. 6 wèi nánshēng shì Shíchuān Yīláng, Huáng Jiāyǒu, Jīn
男生，6位女生。6位男生是石川一郎、黄家友、金
Shíyuán, Zhào Shūzhēn, Dàwèi hé Mǎkè, 6 wèi nǚshēng shì Chén Xīnyí, Sūshān, Ānnà,
时元、赵书真、大卫和马克，6位女生是陈心宜、苏珊、安娜、

10 座位在哪里？ *Finding the Seats*

Hézǐ, Ān Lìxiù hé Xiǎoxuě.
和子、安丽秀和小雪。

Zhào Shūzhēn de zuǒbian shì Huáng Jiāyǒu, hòubian shì Dàwèi; Sūshān de hòubian
赵书真的左边是黄家友，后边是大卫；苏珊的后边
shì Jīn Shíyuán; Ān Lìxiù de zuǒbian shì Chén Xīnyí, yòubian shì Mǎkè; Hézǐ de
是金时元；安丽秀的左边是陈心宜，右边是马克；和子的
yòubian shì Qián Xiǎoxuě. Qǐng nǐ bǎ tāmen de míngzi xiě zài biǎogé zhōng.
右边是钱小雪。请你把他们的名字写在表格中。

	Zhào Shūzhēn 赵书真	Sūshān 苏珊
Shíchuān Yīláng 石川一郎		
	Ān Lìxiù 安丽秀	
Ānnà 安娜	Hézǐ 和子	Qián Xiǎoxuě 钱小雪

留学生 *n.* overseas student
男生 *n.* boy
女生 *n.* girl
左边 *n.* left

后边 *n.* the place behind
右边 *n.* right
表格 *n.* table, form

文天天读 Reading China

语言点 Language Points

有 there be

1. 班上有12位同学。

    "有",动词。表示事物存在。

    "有" is a verb, which means "there be".

    (1) 我家有三口人,爸爸、妈妈和我。

    (2) 杭州有漂亮的西湖,北京有美丽的北海。

请 please, request, ask

2. 请你把他们的名字写在表格中。

    "请",动词。表示客气地希望对方做某事。

    "请" is a verb, which is used to politely ask somebody to do something.

    (1) 小乐请芳芳吃饭了吗?

    (2) 请进,请坐,请喝茶。

练习 Exercises

1. 判断正误。True or false.

    (1) 马克的座位在钱小雪前边。　　　　　　　　　　　　　　( )

    (2) 黄家友、赵书真和大卫都在第一排(first row)。　　　　　( )

10 座位在哪里？ Finding the Seats

2. 选择正确答案。 Choose the correct answer.

（1）钱小雪是（　　）的留学生。

    A. 北京大学　　　　　B. 南京大学　　　　　C. 上海大学

（2）（　　）都是男生。

    A. 赵书真、大卫、和子　　B. 黄家友、大卫、马克　　C. 安娜、小雪、金时元

小知识 Cultural Tips

六朝古都——南京
The Capital of Six Dynasties in History—Nanjing

　　南京是江苏省省会，她与北京、西安、洛阳并称为"中国四大古都"，有"六朝古都"之称。南京位于长江下游沿岸，是长江下游重要的产业城市和经济中心，也是中国重要的文化教育中心之一。

Nanjing, the capital of Jiangsu Province, is recognized as one of the "Four Great Ancient Capitals of China", with Beijing, Xi'an, and Luoyang as the other three. It is also the capital of six dynasties in history. Located in the lower reaches of the Yangtze River, Nanjing is an important industrial city and economic center in that region, as well as one of the nation's important centers of culture and education.

11 小声一点儿
Xiǎoshēng yìdiǎnr

Hush…

Lèle shì gè ài wánr de háizi. Yìtiān, yǐjīng wǎnshang shí diǎn le, tā
乐乐是个爱玩儿的孩子。一天，已经晚上十点了，他

hái bùxiǎng shuìjiào.
还不想睡觉。

Bàba xiǎng ràng tā zǎodiǎnr xiūxi, jiù shuō：“Bàba gěi nǐ jiǎng《Xīyóu Jì》de
爸爸想让他早点儿休息，就说：“爸爸给你讲《西游记》的

gùshi, hǎo bu hǎo?" Lèle zuì xǐhuan tīng 《Xīyóu Jì》 le, tā fēicháng gāoxìng.
故事，好不好？"乐乐最喜欢听《西游记》了，他非常高兴。

11 小声一点儿 Hush...

Yí gè xiǎoshí yǐhòu, fángjiān lǐ fēicháng
一个小时以后，房间里非常
ānjìng, méiyǒu rén shuōhuà le.
安静，没有人说话了。

Māma xiǎng, Lèle kěndìng shuìzháo le.
妈妈想，乐乐肯定睡着了。

Tā dǎkāi Lèle de fángmén, wèn: "Shuìzháo le
她打开乐乐的房门，问："睡着了
ma?"
吗？"

"Bàba shuìzháo le, xiǎoshēng yìdiǎnr."
"爸爸睡着了，小声一点儿。"

玩儿 *v.* play	安静 *adj.* quiet
睡觉 *v.* sleep	肯定 *adv.* to be sure, surely
休息 *v.* sleep	睡着 *v.* fall asleep
讲 *v.* tell	打开 *v.* open
故事 *n.* story	

中文天天读 Reading China

语言点 Language Points

爱 love, be fond of

1. 乐乐是个爱玩儿的孩子。

   "爱",动词。表示非常喜欢,爱好。

   "爱" is a verb, which means to like something very much or enjoy doing something very much.

   (1) 我爱吃外婆做的中国菜。
   (2) 我爱打羽毛球,是个"羽毛球迷"。

一点儿 a little bit

2. 爸爸睡着了,小声一点儿。

   "一点儿",数量短语。用在形容词或某些动词后边,表示程度低,差别小。

   "一点儿" is a numeral-classifier phrase, which often follows adjectives or some verbs and means "slightly" or "to a small degree".

   (1) 这件衣服太小了,我想要大一点儿的。
   (2) 我很想早一点儿去上海旅行。

练习 Exercises

1. 判断正误。True or false.

   (1) 乐乐喜欢听《西游记》的故事。　　　　　　　　　　　　(　　)
   (2) 爸爸给乐乐讲故事的时候,乐乐睡着了。　　　　　　　　(　　)

2. 选择正确答案。Choose the correct answer.

（1）爸爸为什么给乐乐讲故事？（　　）。

　　A. 爸爸喜欢讲故事　　B. 想让乐乐早点儿睡　　C. 妈妈没时间给乐乐讲故事

（2）妈妈开门的时候，（　）睡着了。

　　A. 没有人　　　　　　B. 乐乐　　　　　　　　C. 爸爸

小知识　Cultural Tips

《西游记》
Journey to the West

　　《西游记》是中国"四大名著"之一。小说中讲了孙悟空、猪八戒和沙和尚保护师傅唐僧西天取经、历经九九八十一难的故事。《西游记》在中国深受人们的喜爱，在韩国、日本等国也有较大的影响。

　　Journey to the West is esteemed as one of the "Four Great Classical Novels" of Chinese literature. It tells the story of a Buddhist monk Xuanzang, accompanied by his three disciples and protectors—namely, Sun Wukong, Zhu Bajie and Sha Wujing—travelled to the "Western Regions" to obtain Buddhist sutras, and they finally succeeded after fighting against the eighty-one disasters they encountered on the journey. *Journey to the West* is widely loved in China, and has considerable influence in the Republic of Korea, Japan and other countries.

12 走错了
Zǒu cuò le
The Wrong Door

马东言是我的好朋友,最近他们家的一个水龙头坏了,可是修理工一直没来。

昨天上午9点,有人敲门。马东言的妈妈打开门,是一位修理工!她高兴地说:"太好了,您终于来了。

12 走错了 The Wrong Door

我们已经等您三天了!"

"对不起,我走错了。有一家已经等我一个月了,现在我得去那家!"

水龙头 *n.* water tap	一直 *adv.* all along	对不起 sorry
坏 *v.* break down	敲门 knock at the door	得 *v.* have to
修理工 *n.* repairman		

语言点 Language Points

最近 recently

1. 最近他们家的一个水龙头坏了，可是修理工一直没来。

   "最近"，名词。表示离说话时的时间不长。

   "最近" is a noun, referring to a time not long ago.

   （1）他最近去杭州旅行了，花了不少钱。

   （2）最近我很忙，希望能休息几天。

打开 open, turn on

2. 马东言的妈妈打开门，是一位修理工！

   "打开"，动词。通过某种动作使关闭着的东西开开或机器等工作，"开"是结果。

   "打开" is a verb, which means to make something closed open or machine work. "开" expresses the result.

   （1）现在有羽毛球比赛（match），快打开电视！

   （2）妈妈打开乐乐的房门，看见爸爸已经睡着了。

练习 Exercises

1. 判断正误。True or false.

   （1）马东言和妈妈等了修理工一个月。　　　　　　　　　　　　　　（　　）

   （2）修理工要先给别人修，然后才给马东言家修。　　　　　　　　　（　　）

12 走错了 The Wrong Door

2. 选择正确答案。Choose the correct answer.

（1）修理工（　　）以后才来马东言家。

　　A. 一个月　　　　　　B. 三天　　　　　　　C. 昨天

（2）哪一个和"现在我得去那家"中的"得"一样 (same)？（　　）。

　　A. 我考试得了100分　　B. 他汉字写得很好　　C. 很晚了，我得回家了

小知识 Cultural Tips

钟点工
Hourly Workers

钟点工是指按小时给工资的一种用工形式。现在中国的城市家庭，越来越多地请钟点工帮忙干活儿。钟点工的种类也越来越多，有育婴嫂、保洁员和家庭教师等等。

An hourly worker is an employee paid an hourly wage for his/her services. In China, a growing number of families in cities hire hourly workers of more and more types, such as nursery maids, house cleaners, and home tutors.

13 手机丢了
Lost Mobile Phone

一

寻诺基亚5230黑色手机，这是女朋友送我的生日礼物，对我来说，非常重要。请尽快跟我联系，电话：1283692378，非常感谢！

张 果果

2010年6月27日

13 手机丢了 Lost Mobile Phone

二 Èr

6月26号下午我在学校打篮球时,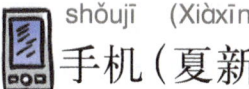手机(夏新A310)放在地上,走的时候忘了。因为上面有很多重要的电话,所以希望捡到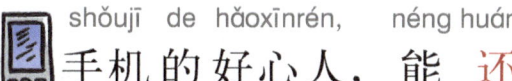手机的好心人,能还给我。我会请客哦(有美女和帅哥同学一起哦☺)。联系电话:88811209。

李 书晴

2010 年 6 月 27 日

丢 *v.* lose	重要 *adj.* important	请客 *v.* invite sb. to dinner
寻 *v.* look for	篮球 *n.* basketball	帅哥 *n.* handsome boy
黑色 *n.* black	捡 *v.* pick up, find	因为……所以 because...
礼物 *n.* gift, present	还 *v.* return	

语言点 Language Points

尽快
as soon as possible

1. 请尽快跟我联系。

   "尽快",副词。表示用最快的速度做某事。

   "尽快" is an adverb, which means to do something as soon as possible.

   (1) 我家的水龙头坏了,请尽快来修理。
   (2) 这件事很重要,请尽快打电话给我。

联系
contact, get/be in touch (with)

2. 请尽快跟我联系。

   "联系",动词。表示一方跟其他方面建立起关系。

   "联系" is a verb, which means to establish relationship with others.

   (1) 大学毕业后,我们就没联系过。
   (2) 想去上海旅行的同学,请跟我联系。

练习 Exercises

1. 判断正误。True or false.

   (1) 张果果的手机是红色的。   (   )
   (2) 李书晴的手机是打篮球时丢的。   (   )

2. 选择正确答案。Choose the correct answer.

(1) 张果果的手机是（　　）送的。

　　A. 父母　　　　　　　B. 朋友　　　　　　　C. 女朋友

(2) 李书晴的手机很重要，因为手机（　　）。

　　A. 是他女朋友送的　　B. 是他的生日礼物　　C. 上面有很多重要的电话

小知识 Cultural Tips

手机在中国
Mobile Phones in China

1987年广州成立了中国第一个移动电话局，有了第一个手机用户。与现在不同的是，因为当时有手机的人很少，所以拥有手机是一种身份的象征。到2010年，中国的手机用户超过7亿，平均不到两个人就有一部。

In the year 1987, China set up its first mobile phone network in the city of Guangzhou, and the first mobile phone in China was registered. What is different from today, though, is that a mobile phone would indicate its owner's high social status, as they were rare then. Yet by the year 2010, the number of mobile phone users in China had reached over 700 million, that is, less than two persons on average owned a mobile phone.

14 古老的城市——西安

Gǔlǎo de chéngshì —— Xī'ān

The Ancient City of Xi'an

昨天晚上九点十分，我和韩国朋友赵京美一起，从北京坐火车去西安旅行。今天早上七点，我们到了西安。

西安是一个古老的城市，非常漂亮。西安最有名的是兵马俑，它们已经在地下2,000多年了。

14 古老的城市——西安 The Ancient City of Xi'an

Bīngmǎyǒng fēicháng duō, wǒ pāile hěnduō zhàopiàn, yǒu chē, yǒu mǎ, háiyǒu shìbīng.
兵马俑 非常 多，我 拍了 很多 照片，有 车、有 马、还有 士兵。

Xī'ān de xiǎochī yě hěn yǒumíng. Zài xiǎochī jiē, wǒmen chīle miàntiáo hé yángròu pàomó. Zhào Jīngměi shì gè měishíjiā, tā yìzhí shuō "hǎo chī! zhēn hǎo chī!"
西安 的 小吃 也 很 有名。在 小吃 街，我们 吃了 面条 和 羊肉 泡馍。赵 京美 是 个 美食家，她 一直 说 "好吃！真 好吃！"

Wǒmen dōu hěn xǐhuan Xī'ān.
我们 都 很 喜欢 西安。

兵马俑 *n.* Terracotta Warriors and Horses
地下 *n.* underground
拍 *v.* take (a picture)
照片 *n.* photo, picture
士兵 *n.* soldier, warrior

小吃 *n.* snack, local delicacy
面条 *n.* noodle
羊肉泡馍 *n.* Pita Bread Soaked in Lamb Soup
美食家 *n.* gourmet

语言点 Language Points

和……一起
together with

1. 我和韩国朋友赵京美一起，从北京坐火车去西安旅行。

    "和……一起"，表示"和……一块儿"。

    "和……一起" means "together with...".

    (1) 李美子喜欢中国菜，她常常和朋友一起做饭。

    (2) 暑假的时候，我喜欢和朋友一起旅行。

最
most

2. 西安最有名的是兵马俑。

    "最"，副词。表示通过在某个范围里比较，性质超过所有同类的。

    "最" is an adverb, which means to have the greatest amount of a particular quality in a certain range.

    (1) 西安最有名的小吃是羊肉泡馍。

    (2) 星期天，西川最喜欢骑自行车出去玩了。

练习 Exercises

1. 判断正误。True or false.

    (1) 我和赵京美坐飞机去西安旅行。　　　　　　　　　　　　( )

    (2) 兵马俑已经在地下很长时间了。　　　　　　　　　　　　( )

14 古老的城市——西安 The Ancient City of Xi'an

2. 选择正确答案。Choose the correct answer.

（1）西安最有名的是（　　）。

    A. 兵马俑　　　　　B. 羊肉泡馍　　　　C. 面条

（2）"美食家"的意思是（　　）。

    A. 吃得很多的人　　B. 喜欢小吃的人　　C. 很会品尝（taste）美食的人

小知识　Cultural Tips

兵马俑
The Terracotta Warriors and Horses

秦始皇是第一个统一中国的皇帝，他的陵墓在西安城东30公里。1974年2月，当地农民在秦始皇陵东侧1.5公里处偶然发现了与真人真马一样大小的兵马俑。从此，一个埋藏了两千多年的地下军阵被挖掘出来，并建成博物馆，这被称为"世界第八大奇迹"。

Emperor Qin Shi Huang, the founding Emperor of the Qin Dynasty, is the first to unify China in history. His tomb was built 30 kilometers east of Xi'an today. In February, 1974, some farmers happened to dig out some life-sized Terracotta Warriors and Horses 1.5 kilometers east of the tomb. After further excavation, a great terracotta army that had been buried for over 2,000 years was unearthed, and the Museum of Terracotta Warriors and Horses was built. The Terracotta Warriors and Horses are regarded as the "Eighth Wonder of the World".

15 漂亮的一"点"
Piàoliang de yì "diǎn"
The Highlight

王羲之是古代著名的书法家。

他的儿子王献之七八岁的时候开始学书法。几年以后，很多人说他的字不错。

一天，献之把很多写好的字给爸爸看。爸爸一边看，一边摇头。

15 漂亮的一"点" The Highlight

看到一个"大"字的时候，非常满意，就在"大"字下面加了一个点。献之又拿给妈妈看。妈妈一边看，一边说："这个'、'写得最好。"献之听了妈妈的话，很不好意思。他不再骄傲，努力练习，后来也成了著名的书法家。

著名 *adj.* famous, well-known
书法家 *v.* calligrapher
给……看 *v.* show something to
一边……一边 *v.* ...while...

摇头 *v.* shake head
加 *v.* add
不好意思 *v.* embarrassed, ashamed
骄傲 *v.* proud, conceited

语言点 Language Points

成
become, turn into

1. 他不再骄傲，努力练习，后来也成了著名的书法家。

   "成"，动词。表示从一种情况、状态变成另一种情况、状态。

   "成" is a verb, which means to turn from one condition or quality to another.

   (1) 10年以后，她成了一名小学教师。

   (2) 1个月后，我们班的同学都成了好朋友。

满意
satisfied

2. 看到一个"大"字的时候，非常满意。

   "满意"，形容词。表示满足自己的愿望；符合自己的心意。

   "满意" is an adjective, which means to be pleased because something has happened in the way you want or because you have got what you want.

   (1) 我的女朋友很漂亮，爸爸妈妈都非常满意。

   (2) 逛了一天，她终于买到了自己满意的衣服。

练习 Exercises

1. 判断正误。True or false.

   (1) 王献之的爸爸是一位著名的书法家。　　　　　　　　　　　　　（　　）

   (2) 爸爸对儿子的字都很满意。　　　　　　　　　　　　　　　　　（　　）

2. 选择正确答案。Choose the correct answer.

(1) "大"字下面加上一点是（　　）。

　　A. 犬　　　　　B. 太　　　　　C. 不

(2) 妈妈认为献之的（　　）写得最好。

　　A. 大　　　　　B. 太　　　　　C. 大字下面的"、"

小知识 Cultural Tips

中国书法
Chinese Calligraphy

书法是中国特有的一种传统艺术。书法一般是指用毛笔书写汉字的方法和规律。中国人使用毛笔书写汉字有很长的历史，只是近一百多年来，人们才开始普遍使用钢笔写字。

Calligraphy is a unique traditional form of art in China, which usually refers to the way and law of ink brush writing. China has a long history of ink brush writing, and it is only nearly 100 years since pens became popular.

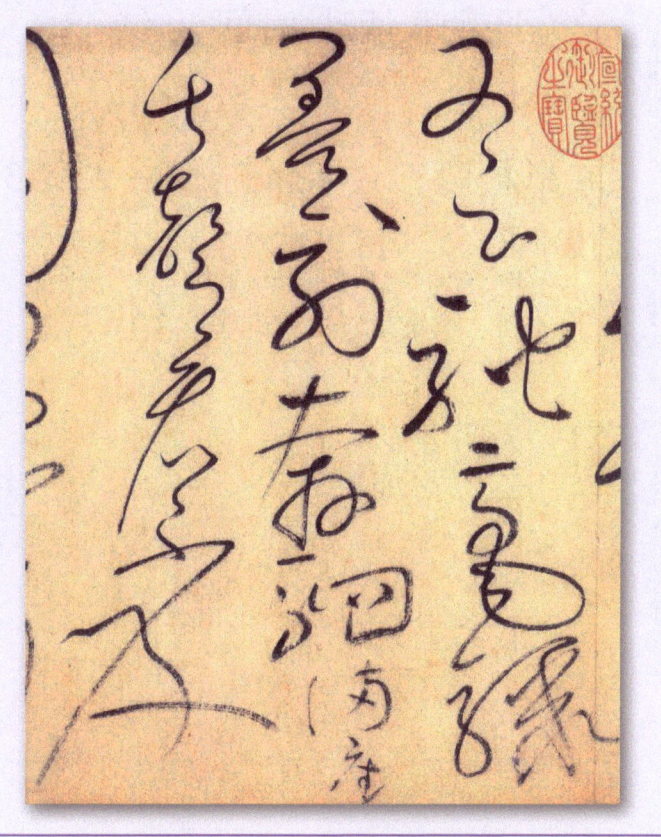

16 通知 Tōngzhī
Notice

Dàjiā hǎo!
大家好！

Yǔmáoqiú huódòng shíjiān wéi měi gè Xīngqī'èr、sì xiàwǔ 4:00—6:00,
羽毛球 活动 时间 为 每个 星期二、四 下午 4：00—6：00，

měi gè Xīngqīsān zhōngwǔ 12:30—13:30.
每个 星期三 中午 12：30—13：30。

Huìfèi měi rén měi nián 30 yuán, yònglái mǎi yǔmáoqiú, qǐng jiāogěi
会费 每人 每 年 30 元，用来 买 羽毛球，请 交 给

Wáng Lánlan lǎoshī.
王 兰兰 老师。

Xiàgè xīngqī de huódòng shíjiān:
下个 星期 的 活动 时间：

16 通知 Notice

^{3 yuè 16 rì （Xīngqī'èr） xiàwǔ 4:00—6:00, liǎng kuài chǎngdì.}
3月16日（星期二）下午 4:00—6:00，两 块 场地。

^{3 yuè 17 rì （Xīngqīsān） zhōngwǔ 12:30—13:30, yí kuài chǎngdì.}
3月17日（星期三）中午 12:30—13:30，一 块 场地。

^{3 yuè 18 rì （Xīngqīsì） xiàwǔ 4:00—6:00, liǎng kuài chǎngdì.}
3月18日（星期四）下午 4:00—6:00，两 块 场地。

^{Huānyíng cānjiā!}
欢迎 参加！

^{Zhōngwénxì}
中文系

^{2010 nián 3 yuè 14 rì}
2010 年 3 月 14 日

星期 n. week	交 v. give, hand over	场地 n. court
会费 n. membership fee	块 m. piece	系 n. department
用来 v. be used for/to		

语言点 Language Points

每
every, each

1. 会费每人每年 30 元，用来买羽毛球。

   "每"，代词。指全体中的任何一个，强调所有个体都是这样。

   "每" is a pronoun, which refers to all the members of a group of things or people, and emphasizes that every member is the same.

   （1）中国的教师节是每年的 9 月 10 日。

   （2）我喜欢运动，每星期我都去打羽毛球。

欢迎
welcome

2. 欢迎参加！

   "欢迎"，动词。表示非常高兴地迎接或接受。

   "欢迎" is a verb, which means to receive or accept very gladly.

   （1）我的家乡在上海，欢迎大家去旅行。

   （2）今天是我生日，欢迎你们来我家。

练习 Exercises

1. 判断正误。True or false.

   （1）每个星期二、三、四都有羽毛球活动。　　（　　）

   （2）下个星期二的羽毛球活动有两块场地。　　（　　）

2. 填表。Fill in the form.

下个星期羽毛球活动时间

	时间	场地
星期二		
星期三		
星期四		

小知识 Cultural Tips

大学生社团
College Student Communities

中国的大学里有很多学生社团，比如合唱团、舞蹈团、爱心社、天文学会、乒乓球俱乐部、羽毛球协会和登山协会等等，它们极大地丰富了大学生们的生活。

In Chinese colleges and universities, there are many student communities and societies, such as chorus troupes, dance troupes, loving-heart societies, astronomical societies, table-tennis clubs, badminton associations, mountaineers clubs, and many others, which greatly enrich students' college life.

17 Bīngtáng húlu
冰糖葫芦
Sugar-Coated Haws

Wǒ xiǎoshíhou jiù xǐhuan chī
我 小时候 就喜欢吃

bīngtáng húlu.
冰糖 葫芦。

Bā suì nà nián, yǒu yìtiān, wǒ
八岁那 年，有一天，我

zhèngzài jiālǐ zuò zuòyè, Míngming
正在 家里做作业， 明明

názhe yí chuàn bīngtáng húlu guòlai le. Kànzhe
拿着一 串 冰糖 葫芦过来了。看着

hǎo chī de bīngtáng húlu, wǒ tūrán xiǎngchū
好吃的 冰糖 葫芦，我突然 想出

le yí gè zhǔyi.
了一个主意。

17 冰糖葫芦 Sugar-Coated Haws

我拿着冰糖葫芦，问他："这上面有10个山楂，吃了1个还有几个？"我拿下一个山楂放到嘴里。

"9个！""对，明明真聪明！再吃掉1个呢？""8个！"很快，山楂变成了5个。这时，明明看着冰糖葫芦，突然大声地哭起来……

作业 n. homework	拿 v. hold	这时 pron. at this time
串 m. a stick of	嘴 n. mouth	大声 loudly
山楂 n. haw	聪明 adj. clever, bright	哭 v. cry

语言点 Language Points

1. 看着好吃的糖葫芦,我突然想出了一个主意。

   "主意",名词。表示做某件事情的办法。

   "主意" is a noun, which means a plan of doing something.

   (1) 我喜欢北京,可是女朋友在上海工作,我没了主意。

   (2) 男朋友生日快到了,送什么生日礼物呢?帮我想个主意吧。

主意
idea

2. 很快,山楂变成了5个。

   "变成",表示一种事物经过变化成为另一种事物。

   "变成" means one thing changes into another.

   (1) 因为我们是同学,所以很快就变成了好朋友。

   (2) 胖子每天走5公里,3个月后,他变成了瘦子。

变成
become, turn into

练习 Exercises

1. 判断正误。True or false.

   (1) 我八岁的时候开始喜欢吃糖葫芦。　　　　　　　　　　　(　　)

   (2) 我一共吃了6个山楂。　　　　　　　　　　　　　　　　(　　)

17 冰糖葫芦 Sugar-Coated Haws

2. 选择正确答案。Choose the correct answer.

（1）看着好吃的糖葫芦，我想出了一个主意，可以（　　）。

　　A. 吃到明明的糖葫芦　　B. 帮助明明学习　　C. 让明明哭

（2）明明看着糖葫芦，突然大声地哭起来，因为（　　）。

　　A. 他不会回答问题　　B. 糖葫芦只有5个了　　C. 糖葫芦不好吃

小知识 Cultural Tips

北方小吃——冰糖葫芦
Sugar-Coated Haws, a Snack in Northern China

冰糖葫芦是中国北方的传统小吃。特别是冬天，天气变冷，街上就开始卖冰糖葫芦了。冰糖葫芦一般是将山楂用竹签串成串后蘸上麦芽糖稀，糖稀遇风迅速变硬，吃起来又酸又甜，还有点儿冰，很好吃。

Sugar-coated haws are a traditional snack in northern China. They are available throughout the year in the street, particularly in winter, when it turns cold. Sugar-coated haws are usually made by first putting haws on a bamboo stick, and then dipping it into a syrup stewed by sugar and water, which cools down to form a hard layer over the haws. The snack, with the crystalline layer, has a fine taste of sour and sweet.

18 马大哈
Mǎdàhā
A Scatterbrain

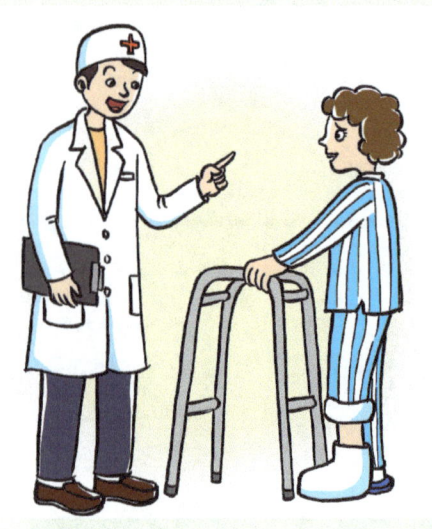

黄家友是个非常聪明的医生，个子很高，长得很帅，工作非常认真。可他在生活中却有点儿马大哈，总是丢东西，特别是丢伞。

他每次出门，只要带伞，回来的时候伞就没了。每次他丢了伞，妻子就会很不高兴。

18 马大哈 A Scatterbrain

Yǒu yìtiān xiàbān huíjiā, Huáng Jiāyǒu názhe yì bǎ sǎn, gāoxìng de duì qīzi shuō:
有一天下班回家，黄家友拿着一把伞，高兴地对妻子说：

"Nǐ kàn, sǎn zài zhèr ne." Qīzi xiàozhe shuō: "Jīntiān nǐ chūqù de shíhou méiyǒu
"你看，伞在这儿呢。"妻子笑着说："今天你出去的时候没有

dài sǎn!"
带伞！"

个子 *n.* height	特别 *adv.* especially
认真 *adj.* concentrated, earnest	伞 *n.* umbrella
总是 *adv.* always	每次 every time
东西 *n.* thing	妻子 *n.* wife

语言点 Language Points

特别
especially, in particular

1. 他总是丢东西,特别是丢伞。

   "特别",副词,表示更进一步。一般用在"是"的前边,构成"特别是……"词组。

   "特别" is an adverb, which means a higher degree or more than usual. It is usually followed by "是", and forms the collocation of "特别是……".

   (1) 我喜欢北京,特别是秋天的北京。
   (2) 他很喜欢运动,特别是打篮球。

只要……就
as long as

2. 他每次出门,只要带伞,回来的时候伞就没了。

   "只要……就",强调如果满足了某个条件,就会产生一定的结果。

   "只要……就" emphasizes that if a certain condition is satisfied, a particular result will occur.

   (1) 我只要有时间,就会去西安看兵马俑。
   (2) 我是个"成龙迷",只要是他的电影,我就会去看。

18 马大哈 A Scatterbrain

练 习 Exercises

1. 判断正误。True or false.

　（1）黄家友在工作中有点儿马大哈。　　　　　　　　　　　　　　（　　）

　（2）黄家友把别人的伞拿回家了。　　　　　　　　　　　　　　　（　　）

2. 选择完成句子。Choose and complete the sentences.

　（1）他工作非常认真，（A. 很少出错 / B. 总是忘记做一些重要的事情）。

　（2）他在生活中有点儿马大哈，（A. 做事很粗心（careless）/ B. 很少丢东西）。

小知识 Cultural Tips

三字俗语
Three-Character Idioms

"三字俗语"指的是三个字的词语，这些词语的意思往往不是它们的本义，也不是字面上的意思。这些词语结构固定，比较口语化，有的表示贬义。如：马大哈（做事粗心大意，马马虎虎的人）；二百五（很笨的人）；纸老虎（看上去很强大，实际上不是）。

A three-character idiom in the Chinese language refers to a group of three-character words that have a special meaning different from their ordinary or literal meaning. These idioms are fixed, colloquial, and sometimes derogatory, such as 马大哈 (a careless person), 二百五 (a stupid person), and 纸老虎 (somebody or something that seems powerful but actually is not).

19 小马过河
Xiǎo mǎ guò hé
A Little Horse Crosses the River

一只小马要过河，可是不知道河水的深浅。他就问老牛："牛爷爷，河水深吗？"老牛说："不深，不深。"

小马来到河边，他刚要过河，小松鼠说："小马，别下去，河水非常深！昨天我的一个朋友就掉进河里了。"

19 小马过河 A Little Horse Crosses the River

Lǎo niú shuō héshuǐ qiǎn, xiǎo sōngshǔ shuō héshuǐ shēn, zěnme bàn? Xiǎo mǎ zhǐhǎo
老牛说河水浅,小松鼠说河水深,怎么办?小马只好

huíjiā wèn māma. Māma hé xiǎo mǎ yìqǐ láidào hé biān, tā ràng xiǎo mǎ zìjǐ shì yi shì.
回家问妈妈。妈妈和小马一起来到河边,她让小马自己试一试。

Xiǎo mǎ shì le shì, héshuǐ bù shēn yě bùqiǎn, tā gāoxìng de guòle hé.
小马试了试,河水不深也不浅,他高兴地过了河。

深 *adj.* deep
浅 *adj.* shallow
松鼠 *n.* squirrel

别 *adv.* do not, had better not
下去 *v.* go down
掉 *v.* fall

中文天天读 Reading China

语言点 Language Points

怎么办
how to deal with it

1. 老牛说河水浅，小松鼠说河水深，**怎么办**？

   "怎么办"，表示询问（处理某事的）方式或者情况。

   "怎么办" is used to ask about the way in which something is done or happens.

   (1) 今天我忘带手机了，怎么办？
   (2) 暑假我想去南京，可是男朋友想去北京，怎么办？

试一试
try

2. 她让小马自己**试一试**。

   "试一试"，表示为了看到效果而做某事，尝试。

   "试一试" means to do something in order to check the result, or to try.

   (1) 衣服需要试一试，才能知道大小。
   (2) 你试一试这个办法吧，它可以帮助你减肥。

练习 Exercises

1. 判断正误。True or false.

   (1) 因为不知道河水深浅，所以小马不敢过河。　　　　　　　　　　　　（　）
   (2) 牛爷爷说河水不深，他是在骗（cheat）小马。　　　　　　　　　　　（　）

2. 选择正确答案。Choose the correct answer.

（1）小马回家问妈妈河水深不深，妈妈让小马（　　）。

　　　A. 自己试一试　　　　B. 问牛爷爷　　　　C. 问小松鼠

（2）（　　）觉得河水很深，因为她的一个朋友昨天掉进河里了。

　　　A. 牛爷爷　　　　　　B. 小松鼠　　　　　　C. 小马

小知识 Cultural Tips

《小马过河》
A Little Horse Crosses the River

　　《小马过河》是浙江一位农村教师在20世纪50年代创作的，它一直被选入中国的小学语文教材。作为世界著名的寓言童话，它还常常被选入各种儿童文学作品集。这个故事告诉我们，对别人的意见不要盲从，要多动脑子去分析，亲自去尝试，才会有正确的认识。

"A Little Horse Crosses the River", written by a teacher in the rural area of Zhejiang Province in the 1950s, has always been in primary school Chinese-teaching textbooks in China. As a world-known fable, it is often selected into collections of children's literature, too. The fable tells us not to blindly follow others' opinions, and real knowledge comes from analysis and practice.

20 一点儿 Yìdiǎnr
Just a Little Bit

Yǒu yí gè wàiguórén, míngzi jiào Mǎkè,
有一个外国人，名字叫马克，

tā jīnnián wǔ shí duō suì le. Yīnwèi gāng dào
他今年五十多岁了。因为刚到

Zhōngguó yí gè yuè, tā hái bú tài huì shuō hànyǔ.
中国一个月，他还不太会说汉语。

Yìtiān tā xiǎng lǐfà, dànshì yòu bù
一天他想理发，但是又不

xīwàng tóufa tài duǎn. Dàole lǐfàdiàn
希望头发太短。到了理发店

yǐhòu, tā yìbiān gēn lǐfàshī shuō
以后，他一边跟理发师说

"yìdiǎnr", yìbiān zuòchū lǐfà de
"一点儿"，一边做出理发的

yàngzi. Lǐfàshī hǎoxiàng tīngdǒng le,
样子。理发师 好像 听懂 了，

yìbiān shuō "OK", yìbiān kāishǐ
一边 说 "OK"，一边 开 始

lǐfà.
理发。

Nàtiān Mǎkè fēicháng lèi, gāng zuòxia
那天马克非常 累，刚 坐下

jiù shuìzháo le. Èr shí fēnzhōng hòu lǐfàshī shuō "OK le", Mǎkè kànzhe jìngzi lǐ de
就 睡着 了。二十 分钟 后理发师说 "OK 了"，马克看着镜子里的

zìjǐ, kūxiào-bùdé. Yīnwèi tā de tóufa zhǐyǒu yìdiǎnr le!
自己，哭笑不得。因为他的头发只有一点儿了！

理发 v. have one's hair cut	理发师 n. hairdresser	累 adj. tired
头发 n. hair	样子 n. gesture	镜子 n. mirror
短 adj. short	懂 v. understand	

语言点 Language Points

1. 理发师好像听懂了。

"好像",副词。表示不很肯定,相当于"似乎"、"大概"。

"好像" is an adverb, which describes the state of not being sure, just as "似乎" or "大概".

(1) 这几天真热,好像到了夏天一样。

(2) 这次考试考得不好,他好像不太高兴。

> **好像**
> seem to, it seems that

2. 马克看着镜子里的自己,哭笑不得。

"哭笑不得",表示哭也不是笑也不是,形容不知道怎么办才好。

"哭笑不得" means not knowing whether to laugh or cry, which is used to express that one does not know what to do.

(1) 杰克把"小心地(dì)滑"看成了"小心地(de)滑",让小明哭笑不得。

(2) 3个月后,胖子打电话问医生怎么回家,医生哭笑不得。

> **哭笑不得**
> do not know whether to cry or laugh

练习 Exercises

1. 判断正误。True or false.

(1) 马克刚到中国一个月,他只会说一点儿汉语。　　　　　　(　)

(2) 理发师明白了马克的意思。　　　　　　　　　　　　　　(　)

2. 选择并完成句子。Choose and complete the sentences.

（1）马克想理发，他（A. 不想头发只有一点儿 / B. 希望头发很短）。

（2）马克看着镜子里的自己，哭笑不得，因为（A. 他很喜欢自己的新发型（hair style）/ B. 他的头发只有一点儿了）。

小知识 Cultural Tips

二月二，龙抬头
Dragon Heads-Raising Day

　　农历二月初二，中国民间普遍认为在这一天理发，会有好运气。因此，民谚说"二月二剃龙头，一年都有精神头儿。"每逢二月二这一天，家家理发店都会来很多顾客，生意非常好。

　　Dragon Heads-raising Day is celebrated every year on the second day of the second month according to the Chinese lunar calendar. There is a belief that a haircut on this day would bring good luck, thus there is a saying that goes "A haircut on Dragon Heads-raising Day ensures vigor throughout the year". Every hairdresser's across China sees one of their busiest days of the year on this day.

21 Qiánmén ≠ qiánménr
前门 ≠ 前门儿
The Tricky Suffix of "R"

Àizǐ shì Rìběn liúxuéshēng,
爱子是日本留学生，

tā hànyǔ xuéde hěn hǎo. Tā hái
她汉语学得很好。她还

hěn xǐhuan yòng érhuàyīn, dànshì
很喜欢用儿化音，但是

yǒu yí cì nàole xiàohua. Nà
有一次闹了笑话。那

yìtiān, Àizǐ xiǎng qù tiān'ānmén fùjìn de qiánmén wánr. Tā zài sùshè
一天，爱子想去天安门附近的前门玩儿。她在宿舍

ménkǒu gēn chūzūchē sījī shuō: "Wǒ yào qù qiánménr."
门口跟出租车司机说："我要去前门儿。"

21 前门 ≠ 前门儿　The Tricky Suffix of "R"

Hěn kuài, sījī gàosu tā: "Qiánménr dào le." Àizǐ hěn qíguài, wèishénme
很快，司机告诉她："前门儿到了。"爱子很奇怪，为什么

zhème kuài ne? Yuánlái, sījī bǎ tā sòngdào le dàxué de qiánménr.
这么快呢？原来，司机把她送到了大学的前门儿。

儿化音 r-ending retroflexion
闹笑话 make a fool of oneself, make a stupid mistake
前门 n. Qianmen/front gate
宿舍 n. dormitory

门口 n. gate, doorway
出租车 n. taxi
司机 n. driver
很快 adv. in a short time

语言点 Language Points

附近
near, neighboring

1. 那一天，爱子想去天安门附近的前门玩儿。

   "附近"，名词。表示不远的地方。

   "附近" is a noun, which refers to a place not far away.

   (1) 请问，学校附近有邮局吗？

   (2) 她家就在附近，骑自行车10分钟。

这么
so, such, like this

2. 爱子很奇怪，为什么这么快呢？

   "这么"，代词，这样。指人或事物的性质、状态、方式、程度等，和"那么"相对。

   "这么", meaning 这样, is a pronoun, which refers to somebody's or something's quality, condition, manner, degree, etc. It is opposite to "那么".

   (1) 西安有这么好的小吃，我还要来！

   (2) 减肥这么难，我不想减肥了。

练习 Exercises

1. 判断正误。True or false.

   (1) 爱子不知道"前门"和"前门儿"的意思不一样。　　　　　　　　　（　　）

   (2) 司机以为爱子要去大学的前门儿。　　　　　　　　　　　　　　（　　）

2. **选择和划线部分意思最相近的选项。** Choose the similar meaning.

（1）她还很喜欢用儿化音，但是有一次<u>闹了笑话</u>。

    A．开个玩笑　　B．说个笑话　　　　C．做了尴尬（embarrassing）的事情

（2）爱子<u>很奇怪</u>，为什么这么快呢？

    A．很少见　　B．觉得很不正常（weird）　　C．很特别

小知识　Cultural Tips

天安门广场
Tian'anmen Square

    天安门广场在北京的市中心，是世界上最大的城市广场之一。它南北长 880 米，东西宽 500 米，面积有 44 万平方米，100 万人可以同时在这里集会。天安门城楼在广场的北面，它是中华人民共和国的象征。

    Tian'anmen Square, one of the largest city squares in the world, is situated in the center of Beijing. It is 880 meters from north to south and 500 meters from east to west, with a total area of 440,000 square meters, and can hold one million people for public celebration or gatherings. To the north of the square sits Tian'anmen Rostrum, which is the symbol of the People's Republic of China.

22 多变的气候
Duōbiàn de qìhòu
A Varied Climate

中国南方和北方的气候很不一样，特别是冬天，温度的差别很大。所以，北方人在看雪的时候，南方人可能在海边游泳。

在冬天，同一天的中午12点，哈尔滨的温度是 -30℃，广州却可能是 20℃，温度的差别有 50℃。

22 多变的气候 A Varied Climate

有趣的是，在同一个地方，早晨和中午温度的差别也可能有30℃，夏天的吐鲁番就是这样的地方。

那里的早晨特别冷，人们要穿很多衣服。中午又变得很热，要穿夏天的衣服。所以，如果你去吐鲁番旅行，一定要多带点儿衣服。

南方 n. south	海边 beach	同 adj. the same
气候 n. climate	有趣 adj. interesting	穿 v. wear, put on
温度 n. temperature		

文天天读 Reading China

语言点 Language Points

差别 difference

1. 南方和北方的冬天，温度的差别很大。

   "差别"，名词。意思是事物之间的不同之处。

   "差别" is a noun, which refers to the difference between things.

   (1) 20年前的中国和现在的中国差别很大。

   (2) 日语和英语差别很大。

旅行 travel, take a trip

2. 如果你去吐鲁番旅行，一定要多带点儿衣服。

   "旅行"，动词。为办事、游览等到较远的外地去。

   "旅行" is a verb, which means to go to places far away for business or sightseeing.

   (1) 明年我想去法国旅行。

   (2) 下星期我准备去云南旅行。

练习 Exercises

1. 判断正误。True or false.

   (1) 冬天，哈尔滨和广州的温差非常大。　　　　　　　　　　（　）

   (2) 夏天的吐鲁番，早晨很热。　　　　　　　　　　　　　　（　）

22 多变的气候 *A Varied Climate*

2. 选择正确答案。Choose the correct answer.

（1）冬天的时候，中国南方人可能去（　　）。

　　A. 看雪　　　　　B. 游泳　　　　　C. 滑雪

（2）夏天在吐鲁番，早上要穿（　　）。

　　A. 很多衣服　　　B. 夏天的衣服　　　C. 春天的衣服

小知识　Cultural Tips

早穿皮袄午穿纱，晚抱火炉吃西瓜
Wearing Fur Jacket in the Morning, Gauze at Noon, and Eating Watermelons Around the Stove in the Evening

这句话的意思是"早上穿厚厚的皮袄，中午却要穿薄薄的纱衣，晚上比较冷，所以要抱着火炉吃西瓜。"这种现象在中国的西北地区特别常见。之所以这样，是因为那儿到处都是沙石，白天的沙石温度升得很快，晚上降温也非常快。

"Wearing fur jacket in the morning, gauze at noon, and eating watermelons around the stove in the evening because of low temperature" describes a common phenomenon in northwest China. This is because it is covered with sand and stones everywhere, whose temperature rises in the day and drops in the night very quickly.

23 Chángshēngguǒ
长生果
Elixir of Life

Zhōngguó gǔdài, yǒu rén gěi huángdì
中国 古代，有人给 皇帝
sòngle yì kē chángshēngguǒ, shuō chīle
送了一颗 长生果，说吃了
zhè kē chángshēngguǒ jiù kěyǐ bù
这颗 长生果 就可以不
sǐ. Yǒu gè rén zhīdào hòu, tōutōu
死。有个人知道后，偷偷
bǎ chángshēngguǒ chī le.
把 长生果 吃了。

23 长生果 Elixir of Life

皇帝非常生气，要杀死他。他一点儿也不害怕，对皇帝说："如果长生果是真的，那我就不会死；如果我死了，那长生果一定不是真的。"皇帝觉得他很聪明，就没有杀他。

古代 *n.* ancient times	杀 *v.* kill
皇帝 *n.* emperor	害怕 *v.* be afraid, be scared
颗 *m.* usually for things small and roundish	真 *adj.* real, genuine
死 *v.* die	

语言点 Language Points

1. 一个人知道后，偷偷把长生果吃了。

   "偷偷"，副词。形容行动不使人觉察。

   "偷偷" is an adverb, which means to do something without anybody else knowing about it.

   (1) 她没去上课，而是偷偷地去看成龙了。

   (2) 他不想学习，偷偷地跑出去玩儿了。

偷偷
stealthily, covertly

2. 他一点儿也不害怕。

   "一点儿也不"，用在形容词或动词前面，表示完全的否定。

   "一点儿也不" is often followed by adjectives or verbs, and it expresses complete negation.

   (1) 这件事我一点儿也不知道，你问别人吧。

   (2) 冬天北京的教室里有暖气（central heating），一点儿也不冷。

一点儿也不
not at all, not a bit

练习 Exercises

1. 判断正误。True or false.

   (1) 吃了长生果可以不死。　　　　　　　　　　　　　　　　（　）

   (2) 那个人是故意（intentionally）吃了长生果的。　　　　　（　）

   (3) 那个人觉得皇帝很聪明。　　　　　　　　　　　　　　　（　）

23 长生果 Elixir of Life

2. 选择并完成句子。 Choose and complete the sentences.

(1) 那个人一点儿也不害怕，因为（A. 他知道皇帝不会杀他 / B. 长生果是假的）。

(2) 皇帝后来没有杀他，因为（A. 如果他死了，长生果就是假的 / B. 皇帝还有长生果）。

小知识 Cultural Tips

秦始皇
Emperor Qin Shi Huang

秦始皇（公元前259年—公元前210年），是中国第一个封建王朝——秦王朝的始皇帝。对于中国的统一，秦始皇的功绩是前无古人的，如统一文字、修建长城等。另外历史上还留下了不少关于他寻找神仙、求取仙药的故事，说他出巡总是到海边去，因为他听说神仙总是在海边出现。

Emperor Qin Shi Huang (259 BC – 210 BC), is the first emperor of the Qin Dynasty, the first feudal empire in Chinese history. Besides his unprecedented achievement of building a united China, he also unified the Chinese characters in writing, built the Great Wall, etc. There are also stories in history about his searching for immortal beings and the fabled elixir of life, which have it that he often took his tours of inspection to the seaside, for it was said that immortal beings would appear there.

24 我看见了大熊猫
Wǒ kànjiàn le dàxióngmāo

Seeing Pandas

2010年8月8日 星期六 晴

今天我们和丁老师一起去北京动物园了,这是我来中国以后第一次参观动物园。我们是坐公共汽车去的,北京的车票特别便宜,只要四毛钱。

24 我看见了大熊猫 Seeing Pandas

Běijīng Dòngwùyuán fēicháng dà,
北京 动物园 非常 大，

lǐmiàn yǒu hěn duō dòngwù. Wǒ zuì
里面 有 很 多 动物。我 最

xǐhuan de dāngrán shì dàxióngmāo le,
喜欢 的 当然 是 大熊猫 了，

jīntiān wǒ yí cì jiù kànjiàn le liù zhī dàxióngmāo, tāmen tài kě'ài le!
今天我一次就 看见了六只 大熊猫，她们太可爱了！

Xià gè yuè wǒ de nánpéngyou lái
下个月我的 男朋友 来

Běijīng, tā yě hěn xǐhuan dàxióngmāo,
北京，他也很 喜欢 大熊猫，

wǒ hái huì hé tā yìqǐ zài qù cānguān
我还会和他一起再去 参观

Běijīng Dòngwùyuán.
北京 动物园。

动物园 n. zoo
参观 v. visit
公共汽车 n. bus

车票 n. ticket
当然 adv. surely, certainly

可爱 adj. lovely, cute
男朋友 n. boyfriend

107

文天天读 Reading China

语言点 Language Points

1. 北京的车票特别便宜，只要四毛钱。

   便宜
   cheap, low in price

   "便宜"，形容词。表示价格很低。

   "便宜" is an adjective, which means something is low in price.

   (1) 她买的衣服很便宜，也很好看。

   (2) 这是女朋友送我的生日礼物，虽然便宜，但是很重要。

2. 今天我一次就看见了六只大熊猫，她们太可爱了！

   太……了
   so..., too...

   "太……了"，表示程度过分或者很高。

   "太……了" means in a high degree.

   (1) 今天38℃，太热了！

   (2) 听到这个好消息，我真是太高兴了。

练习 Exercises

1. 判断正误。True or false.

   (1) 今天是我来中国以后第一次看见大熊猫。　　　　　　　　（　）

   (2) 北京的公共汽车票很便宜。　　　　　　　　　　　　　　（　）

   (3) 我的男朋友这个月来北京。　　　　　　　　　　　　　　（　）

2. 选择并完成句子。Choose and complete the sentences.

（1）我太喜欢大熊猫了，下个月我还要（A. 参观 / B. 学习）动物园。

（2）动物园的门票淡季（dànjì, off-season）特别（A. 贵 / B. 便宜），一张10元。

小知识 Cultural Tips

北京动物园
Beijing Zoo

北京动物园是中国开放最早、饲养动物最多的动物园之一，已有100多年的历史。园内动物有450余种4500多只，海洋鱼类及海洋生物500余种10000多尾。每年接待中外游客600多万人次。

Beijing Zoo, with a history of over 100 years, is one of the oldest zoos in China and has one of the largest animal collections in the country. The zoo is home to more than 4,500 land animals of over 450 species, as well as over 10,000 marine animals of more than 500 species, and receives more than 6 million visitors from home and abroad each year.

25 我开博客了
Starting a Blog

我叫高希希,来中国已经半年了,去了很多地方旅游。朋友们知道后,都很羡慕,希望我发一些照片给他们。有朋友说:"你开一个博客(blog)吧,把你看到的中国拍出来,让我们也看一看。"我觉得这是一个好主意,所以今天我开博客了(http://blog.sina.com.cn/zhubrook),欢迎你们!

25 我开博客了 Starting a Blog

Zuótiān wǒ qùle Zhōngguó zuì yǒumíng de dàxué —— Běijīng Dàxué, suǒyǐ wǒ de
昨天 我 去了 中国 最 有名 的大学——北京大学，所以我的

dì-yī piān bókè jiù shì "měilì de Běidà".
第一篇博客就是"美丽的北大"。

半年 half a year	让 *v.* let	篇 *m.* piece
发 *v.* send	有名 *adj.* well-known	美丽 *adj.* beautiful

中文天天读 Reading China

语言点 Language Points

羡慕
envy

1. 朋友们知道后，都很羡慕，希望我发一些照片给他们。

"羡慕"，动词。表示非常希望自己也能有别人那样的才能、优点或条件。

"羡慕" is a verb, which means to wish oneself had somone else's abilities, strong points or conditions.

(1) 他的字写得不好，所以他非常羡慕王献之。

(2) 她买了一件非常漂亮的衣服，让我很羡慕。

V.＋出来
finish doing something

2. 你开一个博客（blog）吧，把你看到的中国拍出来。

"V.＋出来"，"出来"用在动词后面，表示通过动作使事物显露或分辨。

In the collocation of "V.＋出来", "出来" follows the verb, and means to make things appear or be distinguished through doing something.

(1) 我喜欢旅行，也喜欢把我去过的地方都拍出来。

(2) 我想开一个博客，把留学的生活写出来。

练 习 Exercises

1. 判断正误。True or false.

(1) 高希希来中国已经6个月了。 （ ）

(2) 高希希很喜欢在中国旅游。 （ ）

(3) 高希希昨天去了北京大学。 （ ）

25 我开博客了 Starting a Blog

2. 选择并完成句子。Choose and complete the sentences.

（1）他家的孩子考上了北京大学，真让人（A. 羡慕 / B. 奇怪）。

（2）朋友建议（jiànyì, advise）我去西藏，我觉得这是个不错的（A. 参观 / B. 主意）。

3. 连线。Match.

开	旅行
拍	博文
去	博客
发	照片

小知识 Cultural Tips

博 客
Blog

"博客"这个词是从英文单词Blog音译而来。写博客的人叫"博主"。博客2000年进入中国后迅速发展，现在很多人的生活已经离不开博客了。中国最有名的博客是新浪博客和搜狐博客。

"博客" is transliterated from the English word "blog". A person who creates and edits the blog is the "blogger". Since its introduction to China in the year 2000, blogs have been expanding rapidly, and have become an indispensable part in many people's daily life. The most well-known blogs in China are Sina Blog and Sohu Blog.

练习答案
Answer Keys

第一课

1. (1) ×　(2) ×
2. (1) B　(2) A

第二课

1. (1) √　(2) ×
2. (1) C　(2) B

第三课

1. (1) ×　(2) √　(3) √
2. (1) A　B　A
   (2) B　A　A

第四课

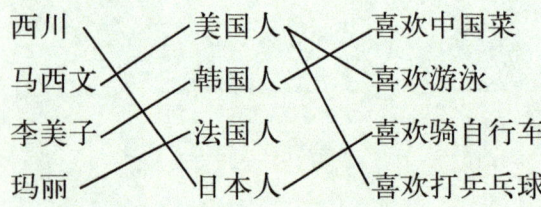

第五课

1. (1) ×　(2) √　(3) √　(4) √
2.

	出生地	居住地
我	美国	美国
妈妈	中国	美国
外婆	中国	中国

第六课

1. (1) ×　(2) √
2. (1) C　(2) C

第七课

1. (1) ×　(2) √
2. (1) B　(2) B

第八课

1. (1) ×　(2) ×
2. (1) B　(2) B　C

第九课

1. (1) ×　(2) √
2. (1) C　(2) B

第十课

1. (1) √　(2) ×
2. (1) B　(2) B

114

第十一课

1. (1) √   (2) ×
2. (1) B   (2) C

第十二课

1. (1) ×   (2) √
2. (1) B   (2) C

第十三课

1. (1) ×   (2) √
2. (1) C   (2) C

第十四课

1. (1) ×   (2) √
2. (1) A   (2) C

第十五课

1. (1) √   (2) ×
2. (1) B   (2) C

第十六课

1. (1) √   (2) √
2.

	时间	场地
星期二	下午4:00—6:00	两块场地
星期三	中午12:30—13:30	一块场地
星期四	下午4:00—6:00	两块场地

第十七课

1. (1) ×   (2) ×
2. (1) A   (2) B

第十八课

1. (1) ×   (2) √
2. (1) A   (2) A

第十九课

1. (1) √   (2) ×
2. (1) A   (2) B

第二十课

1. (1) √   (2) ×
2. (1) A   (2) B

第二十一课

1. (1) √   (2) √
2. (1) C   (2) B

第二十二课

1. (1) √   (2) ×
2. (1) B   (2) A

第二十三课

1. (1) √   (2) √   (3) ×
2. (1) A   (2) A

115

第二十四课

1. (1) √　(2) √　(3) ×

2. (1) A　(2) B

第二十五课

1. (1) √　(2) √　(3) √

2. (1) A　(2) B

3. 开——博客
   拍——照片
   去——旅行
   发——博文

声　明

　　本书所采用的语料，大多来自报刊、杂志、网络。根据本书的特点和需要，我们对所选材料进行了删节和改编。因时间紧迫，部分作者尚未联系上，请作者主动与我们联系，我们将按著作权法有关规定支付稿酬。在此，我们谨对原文作者表示感谢。

中文天天读 Reading China 外研社汉语分级读物

| 978-7-5135-0967-1 | 978-7-5135-0834-6 | 978-7-5600-8234-9 | 978-7-5600-8235-6 |
| 定价 42.00 | 定价 39.00 | 定价 39.00 | 定价 39.00 |

| 978-7-5600-8236-3 | 978-7-5600-8237-0 | 978-7-5600-9117-4 | 978-7-5600-9254-6 | 978-7-5600-9159-4 | 978-7-5135-0311-2 |
| 定价 39.00 | 定价 39.00 | 定价 42.00 | 定价 42.00 | 定价 42.00 | 定价 42.00 |

网址：www.fltrp-clt.com　　电话：010-88819480　　邮箱：lixue@fltrp.com

中文天天读 *Reading China* 外研社汉语分级读物

978-7-5135-0900-8	978-7-5135-0945-9	978-7-5135-0846-9	978-7-5135-0943-5
定价：39.00	定价：39.00	定价：42.00	定价：42.00
978-7-5135-0944-2	978-7-5135-1013-4	978-7-5135-0988-6	978-7-5135-0949-7
定价：39.00	定价：39.00	定价：42.00	定价：42.00

| 978-7-5600-9434-2 | 978-7-5135-0638-0 | 978-7-5600-9545-5 | 978-7-5600-9780-0 |
| 定价：39.00 | 定价：39.00 | 定价：39.00 | 定价：39.00 |

中文天天读包含如下产品

- 爱上中国　　　　　　1A（英语版、日语版、韩语版）　　● 好一朵茉莉花　　　　3B（英语版、日语版、韩语版）
- 小马过河　　　　　　1B（英语版、日语版、韩语版）　　● 北京欢迎你　　　　　4A（英语版、日语版、韩语版）
- 奇妙的中文　　　　　2A（英语版、日语版、韩语版）　　● 种下一棵爱情树　　　4B（英语版、日语版、韩语版）
- 自行车王国　　　　　2B（英语版、日语版、韩语版）　　● 熊猫外交　　　　　　5A（英语版、日语版、韩语版）
- 八月八日，我们结婚　3A（英语版、日语版、韩语版）　　● 中国的"春运潮"　　　5B（英语版、日语版、韩语版）

网址：www.fltrp-clt.com　　电话：010-88819480　　邮箱：lixue@fltrp.com